United States
Department
of Agriculture

Forest Service

**Rocky Mountain
Research Station**

General Technical
Report RMRS-GTR-123

February 2004

Fleas and Lice
of Mammals in
New Mexico

I0439813

Paulette L. Ford

Richard A. Fagerlund

Donald W. Duszynski

Paul J. Polechla

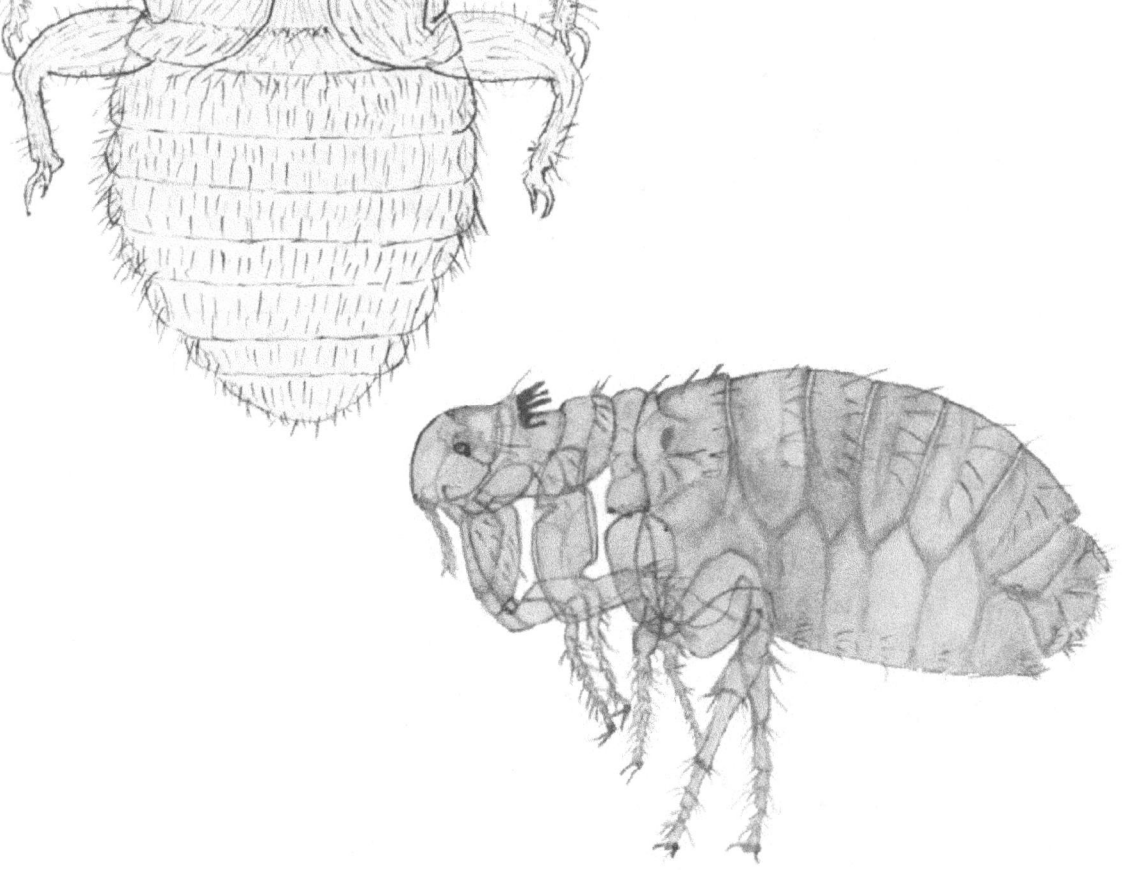

Ford, Paulette L.; Fagerlund, Richard A.; Duszynski, Donald W.; Polechla, Paul J. 2004. **Fleas and lice of mammals in New Mexico.** Gen. Tech. Rep. RMRS-GTR-123. Fort Collins, CO: U.S. Department of Agriculture, Forest Service, Rocky Mountain Research Station. 57 p.

Abstract

All available records are compiled for three orders of ectoparasites of mammals in New Mexico: fleas (Siphonaptera), sucking lice (Anoplura), and chewing lice (Mallophaga). We have drawn from records at the University of New Mexico's Museum of Southwestern Biology, the Vector Control Program of the New Mexico Environment Department, the Environmental Health Department of the City of Albuquerque, and several private collections. We list 99 species of fleas, 27 species of sucking lice, and two species of chewing lice. Included are appendices that list recorded ectoparasite species and their hosts in New Mexico and the counties associated with host ectoparasite infestations. We report at least four new state host records for fleas.

Keywords: Anoplura, chewing lice, ectoparasite, flea, lice, louse, Mallophaga, New Mexico mammalian hosts, Siphonaptera, sucking lice

The Authors

Paulette Ford is a Research Ecologist with the USDA Forest Service, Rocky Mountain Research Station, in Albuquerque, NM. She holds an M.S. in biology from the University of New Mexico and a Ph.D. in Renewable Natural Resources from the University of Arizona. She has worked extensively in Latin America and the American Southwest on research ranging from the systematics of parasites and amphibians to small mammal and amphibian community structures in deserts, grasslands, and tropical deciduous forests. **Richard Fagerlund** is an Integrated Pest Management Coordinator with the University of New Mexico. He currently has a newspaper column in the Albuquerque Tribune on pest control and is the author of four books on insects. **Donald Duszynski** is a Professor of Biology at the University of New Mexico. He has an M.S. and Ph.D. from the Department of Zoology at Colorado State University. He has been at UNM since 1970 and specializes in endoparasites of wild mammals, especially the coccidian or parasitic protists. **Paul Polechla** is a Research Associate Professor at the University of New Mexico in the biology department's Museum of Southwestern Biology Mammal Division. He earned his M.S. at Eastern New Mexico University and his Ph.D. at the University of Arkansas. He was a member of the Southwestern Zoonotic Disease Program (1996-2000) studying hantavirus and deer mice (*Peromyscus maniculatus*) ecology. His interests are mammalian ecology with an emphasis on predator-prey and host-parasite relationships.

cover illustrations by: Johnna Autumn Strange.
Louse (upper), flea (lower).

Contents

Acknowledgments

We wish to thank the following people and institutions: Sandra Brantley for her extensive work with the manuscript and the arthropod collections; Lee Couch for compiling the data, editing, and organizing the final manuscript; Dawn Chen Sun for reviewing the reference material used in the manuscript; Clifford Crawford, Lane Eskew, and Deborah Finch for reviewing multiple drafts of the manuscript and making many valuable suggestions; and Terrence Enk, New Mexico Department of Game and Fish, for specific consultation. Thanks to Ted Brown and Pamela Reynolds, New Mexico Environment Department; New Mexico Environment Department's Vector Control Program; Rudy Bueno, City of Albuquerque Environmental Health Department; Cheryl Parmenter and Kim Heckscher-Decker, Department of Biology, UNM and the Sevilleta Long Term Ecological Research (LTER) Program; Dwayne Salazar, DJ's Pest Control, Albuquerque, NM; and David C. Lightfoot, Sevilleta LTER, Jornada LTER, and Bandelier National Monument for supplying information, specimens, and identifications. We also thank Terry Yates, principal investigator of the small mammal hantavirus studies and Jon Dunnum, Brian Frank, W. Scott Knapp, Kimberly Leuthner, and Todd Meinecke for assistance in trapping small mammals that supplied specimens; Peggy Case for contributing ectoparasites from lagomorphs; and the Bureau of Land Management, the National Institutes of Health, Centers for Disease Control and Prevention (CDC), and the Bureau of Indian Affairs for funding mammal studies that contributed data to this document. This manuscript is dedicated to Michael J. Patrick, assistant professor of biology at Pennsylvania State University, who contributed many of the host animals and flea descriptions that are included in the checklist. Dr. Patrick died 10 March 2000.

Fleas and Lice From Mammals in New Mexico

Paulette L. Ford, Richard A. Fagerlund,
Donald W. Duszynski, and Paul J. Polechla

Introduction

The purpose of this work is to provide baseline data of what is known and can be documented about the fleas and lice of New Mexico mammals. Within that context, we summarize the publications on this topic, document the fleas and lice that are accessioned into the Arthropod Division of the University of New Mexico's Museum of Southwestern Biology (UNM-MSB), and provide some general information about the biology of fleas and lice and the potential disease agents they may transmit to other mammals in New Mexico, including humans. Since infestations of fleas, sucking lice, and chewing lice in humans, domesticated animals, and wildlife may lead to discomfort, debilitating disease, and/or death, this information has implications for, but not limited to, federal, state, and private land managers, scientists, public health officials, and the general public.

New Mexico has the distinction of having one of the highest diversities of land mammals in the United States. There are approximately 150 extant, native mammal species representing eight orders, 25 families, and 71 genera in the state (Frey and Yates 1996). The potential for flea and louse diversity is, therefore, very great. In addition, when non-native mammals are introduced into the state or increase their range(s) from adjacent states, they bring with them their ectoparasites that may be transmitted to endemic species.

In this manuscript we compile all available records for three orders of ectoparasites of mammals in New Mexico: fleas (Siphonaptera), sucking lice (Anoplura), and chewing lice (Mallophaga). There is a lack of information about these ectoparasites, due to the low numbers of the host species studied and to the fact that not all areas of the state have been sampled thoroughly for fleas. Although there is some information on fleas from certain parts of the state, such as Santa Fe County, much less is known about the lice in New Mexico. There are few records of chewing lice from this state's mammals, and most of the recent records of sucking lice have come from small mammal population studies at the Sevilleta National Wildlife Refuge (SNWR) near Socorro, New Mexico.

Of the 150 mammal species in New Mexico that potentially act as host to one or more species of fleas and lice, only 82 are documented to host these ectoparasites. These reports are widespread temporally and geographically, and most represent only one collection event from one locality. A total of 99 species of fleas, 27 species of sucking lice, and two species of chewing lice are known and documented from New Mexico mammals. However, should every mammal species be thoroughly surveyed throughout its known range, the number of flea and lice species on New Mexico mammals would clearly be much higher than this. For example, we already have documented that at least 29 New Mexico mammals have 10 or more species of fleas recorded from them. For these reasons, it is clear that the study of the mammalian fleas and lice parasitizing New Mexico mammals is in need of attention.

Vertebrate biologists, who work in the field in New Mexico, can play a pivotal role in our understanding of the diversity and distribution of ectoparasites infesting this state's mammal (and other terrestrial vertebrate) populations by properly collecting specimens from study animals. The methods for collecting and preserving ectoparasites in the field are simple yet important:

1. Collect the organism(s) from the surface of the host and place them in a vial or other container with 70 percent ethanol or similar alcohol (see Gardner 1996 and Whitaker 1982 for more specific details).
2. Using a No. 2 pencil or indelible (India) ink pen, write the following information on a small label to be placed into the collection vessel: careful and correct identity of the host animal, its precise location of collection, the sex of the animal and its approximate age (juvenile, adult), the date (mm/dd/yy), and your name and collection number (if any).
3. Send or take specimens to the Arthropod Division, UNM-MSB. If possible, the host animal (symbiotype host, see Frey and others 1992; Brooks 1993) should be collected and also taken to the Mammal Division, UNM-MSB, or placed in another accredited museum.

For each of the three orders of ectoparasites covered in this annotated list, we present information on their general biology, their development, diseases they can carry and/or transmit, and the means of controlling them. Mammalian hosts from which we have reliable ectoparasite records are grouped alphabetically by order, and within their order, by family, genus, and species. Under each host species is a list of the specific type of ectoparasites known, the New Mexico counties in which they were collected, the UNM-MSB voucher number if available, any remarks that are appropriate to that parasite or its host, and pertinent reference material(s).

Fleas (Order Siphonaptera)

General

Fleas are small, wingless, hematophagous (blood feeding) insects that are compressed laterally and range in size from about 1 up to several millimeters in length. The head is roughly triangular in shape and usually bears a pair of conspicuous black eyes. The entire body, including legs, is covered with bristles and small spines. Approximately 2,500 species and subspecies belonging to 239 genera have been named to date (Roberts and Janovy 2000; Service 2000). They are all ectoparasites of warm-blooded (homiothermic) vertebrate hosts (birds, mammals), and both male and female adults feed on blood. About 94 percent of known species infest mammals, with the remainder infesting birds. Some fleas are highly specific, known from only one host species (Thomas 1996). However, most flea species have one or two preferred host species, others are more euryxenous (generalists) in their feeding preference and are known to parasitize hosts of a particular genus or family of hosts, and still others are cosmopolitan, feeding on virtually any vertebrate host they should chance upon (Thomas 1996). Conversely, some host species are known to harbor only one flea species while, at the other extreme, a few host species have been found to host more than 50 flea species throughout their range (Thomas 1988).

Fleas, like all insects, have three pairs of legs, but theirs are powerful and specialized for jumping, especially the longer hind legs. Some fleas can jump more than 100 times their body length and/or can execute a standing jump more than 120 times their height. In doing this, they can reach an acceleration of 140 times gravity in little more than a millisecond. How they can accomplish such extraordinary feats is not completely understood (Roberts and Janovy 2000). We do not understand yet the exact necessity of possessing such ability (e.g., avoiding predation, moving from host to host, demonstrating good genes in sexual selection).

Development

Fleas are all holometabolous, i.e., they undergo a complete metamorphosis with (usually) four distinct developmental stages between the egg and the adult. Egg laying behavior of adult fleas is almost always adapted and co-evolved to the behavior of the host upon which it lives (Kim 1985). Usually, females ready to oviposit leave the host to deposit eggs in the host's immediate or general territory (nest or burrow); in a few species, the female remains on the host, but her smooth eggs usually fall to the ground. Off the host, eggs are laid in/near cracks and crevices among dust, dirt, and debris. Generally, eggs hatch in a relatively short period of time (2-21 days), but this depends on environmental conditions (especially rodent burrow temperature and humidity) (Thomas 1996; Roberts and Janovy 2000; Service 2000). The stage that hatches from the egg is called larva (1st instar) because it does not look like the adult; it later will molt twice producing successive instars. Each of the three instars usually requires some blood in its diet, but this is not taken directly from feeding on a host. Rather, they ingest dried feces from adult fleas along with other debris from their immediate environment (fur, feathers) or, in some extreme cases, feed on fecal blood as it passes directly from the anus of their mother or another feeding adult, while they are attached to that adult's abdomen (Thomas 1996). The 3rd instar flea larva will spin a silken cocoon, or pupal case, often embedded with surrounding detritus, and enter the pupal stage. The pupa remains within its case and undergoes metamorphosis to the adult body form; it stays within the cocoon in the adult form--sometimes for weeks, months, or even up to one year--until certain host recognition factors stimulate it to leave the cocoon.

Upon hatching, the adult fleas must take a blood meal before mating and egg production occurs. In some species, certain growth hormones in the blood of the host may trigger the fleas to mate and lay eggs. Under adverse conditions (host absence), adult fleas can survive long periods without food (e.g., in nests, tunnels), especially under conditions of high humidity (Roberts and Janovy 2000). Unlike adults, however, larvae cannot tolerate extremes in relative humidity and will die if the humidity is either too high or too low (Service 2000).

Diseases Carried/Caused/Transmitted

Fleas are primarily a nuisance due to the considerable discomfort, irritation, and annoyance caused by their bites. The most common nuisance flea is the cat flea, *Ctenocephalides felis*. Other fleas of lesser importance are the dog flea, *C. canis*, and the so-called human flea, *Pulex irritans*. Fleas of other domesticated animals may be of local importance. Fleas frequently bite humans on the ankles and legs, but at night during sleep, people may be bitten all over the body. Intense itching may result in a person becoming sensitized, and children usually experience greater discomfort than older persons (Service 2000). Some fleas of wild animals are important vectors of disease; these are summarized below.

Plague

Plague is primarily a disease of wild animals (a zoonosis), especially rodents. Over 200 mammal species have been shown to harbor plague bacteria, with some species being particularly susceptible. Prairie dogs, especially *Cynomys gunnisoni*, are uniformly susceptible to fatal infections with plague, and large proportions (99 percent) or even entire populations have been destroyed in a single epizootic event (Lechleitner and others 1962; Hubbard and Schmitt 1984).

Plague is caused by a bacterium, *Yersinia pestis* (syn. *Pasturella pestis*); it is of Old World origin and throughout history has been referred to as the "Black Death." The profound impact of plague on humans and on human history, more than any other single infectious agent ever, is summarized by Hubbard and Schmitt (1984), Roberts and Janovy (2000), and Marquardt and others (2000).

Plague was first discovered in North America from California ground squirrels (*Spermophilus beecheyi*) in 1905 (Barnes 1982). It was first detected in native New Mexico rodents in 1938 (Laney 1950), and the first documented human case of plague in New Mexico occurred in 1949 (Rollag and others 1981). In the United States, at least 19 different flea species have been found to bite humans, but species in more than 50 genera are important globally as potential vectors of plague. As of 1982, 18 rodent species (two lagomorphs and nine carnivores) were documented to have been infected by plague in New Mexico (Brown, undated). At least 33 species of flea have tested positive as vectors of sylvatic plague in New Mexico (Fagerlund and others 2001).

The normal cycle of plague transmission is between wild rodents and their fleas in nature and is termed sylvatic, campestral, rural, or endemic plague. When plague bacteria are transmitted to rats living in close association with people, such as in rat-infested slums, fleas (particularly, *Xenopsylla cheopis*) that normally feed on rats may turn their attention to humans. Rats infected with plague bacteria may develop acute and fatal septicemia. Upon the death of the host, infected fleas will leave this host and feed on humans.

When fleas ingest bacteria along with blood from infected rodents, the bacteria multiply rapidly in the gut of the flea to the extent that their mass blocks the passage of later blood meals through the flea's proventriculus. Thus, when the flea feeds again, the blood it takes in cannot pass the obstruction, becomes contaminated with bacteria, and is regurgitated back into the bite wound. Interestingly, the ability of various flea species to allow rapid growth of *Y. pestis* organisms that block the gut is a deciding factor of the efficacy of the flea as a good vector (Roberts and Janovy 2000).

Plague manifests itself in humans in one of three forms: bubonic, pneumonic, or septicemic. The most common, bubonic, causes swollen lymph nodes in the groin or armpits. These swellings or "buboes" can get as big as chicken eggs and occur in about 75 percent of all human cases during epidemics. Pneumonic plague occurs when the lungs are heavily involved and produces a pneumonia-like condition that is highly contagious to other humans. Septicemic plague is a generalized blood infection, often with little or no prior lymph node involvement (Roberts and Janovy 2000). Humans become infected with plague by being bitten by a *Yersinia pestis* infected flea or by handling a dead plague infected animal without gloves (NM Dept. of Health, Office of Epidemiology, pers. comm.).

Plague is most common in temperate regions during summer and autumn months and in the tropics during the cooler months. Heat and dryness negatively impact the spread of plague. Campestral plague, that seen in animals of open (rather than wooded) areas, is widespread and common in wild rodents and rabbits of the United States west of the 100th meridian. Human cases in these areas occur only sporadically, often after a person has had contact with wild rodents or rabbits and their fleas. New Mexico has had the highest case rate of human plague in the last decade (Roberts and Janovy 2000). For example, during 1988-2002, a total of 112 human cases of plague were reported from 11 western states. The majority, 97 of the 112 cases (87 percent), were exposed in the four states of Arizona, California, Colorado, and New Mexico, with 48 of the 97 (49 percent) occurring in New Mexico (CDC 2003).

Murine, Flea-Borne or Endemic Typhus

This form of typhus is caused by *Rickettsia typhi* (=*R. mooseri*), which is virtually identical to *R. prowazekii*, the typhus-causing organism transmitted to humans by body lice (see below). When ingested by the flea, the rickettsiae multiply in its gut, but unlike plague bacilli, they do not cause blockage. Rather, infection of the vertebrate host occurs when infected feces from the flea is rubbed into abrasions or comes into contact with mucous membranes. The rickettsial organisms also can be released when fleas are crushed as they are biting, and then, inadvertently, their contaminated body juices are rubbed into wounds. Murine typhus is essentially a disease of murine rodents, especially *Rattus* species; it is common in warm climates and also infects a wide range of other small mammals. Murine typhus is transmitted by various fleas including *Xenopsylla, Nosopsyllus*, and *Leptopsyllus* species, as well as by the rat louse *Polyplax spinulosa* and the tropical rat mite *Ornithonyssus bacoti*. Transovarial transmission, when the rickettsial organism passes from an infected female flea to its ovaries, also occurs to transmit the infection from egg to larva to adult (Service 2000). In humans, the rickettsial organism causes a rather mild, febrile illness that lasts about two weeks, accompanied by headache, chills, body pain, and rash. The disease affects elderly people more severely than it does the young. Interestingly, the opossum (*Didelphis virginiana*), a New Mexico resident (Bermudez and others 1995), also is a reservoir host for murine typhus, and this species is proliferating in many urban and suburban areas, creating the possibility for resurgence of this disease (Roberts and Janovy 2000; Service 2000).

Myxomatosis

This is a disease of rabbits (Order: Lagomorpha) caused by a *Myxoma* virus that was native to South America, but it has spread to the USA and the UK. It is transmitted by a number of blood sucking arthropods including fleas, mites, and mosquitoes. The disease can and has caused considerable losses in the domestic rabbit (*Oryctolagus cuniculus*) industry.

Other Parasites

The flea *Nosopsyllus fasciatus* transmits the non-pathogenic kinetoplastid protist *Trypanosoma lewisi* from rat to rat. Fleas from dogs (*C. canis*), cats (*C. felis*), and humans (*P. irritans*) can serve as intermediate hosts of *Dipylidium caninum*, a tapeworm that is common in cats (*Felis catus*) and dogs (*Canis familiaris*) and can be transmitted to humans, especially children. Certain tapeworms of mice and rats also can be transmitted from host to host: *Nosopsyllus fasciatus* and *X. cheopis* for the rat tapeworm; and *Hymenolepis diminuta, X. cheopis, C. felis, C. canis*, and *P. irritans* for the mouse tapeworm *H. nana*. (*Hymenolepis nana* is a reasonably common parasite of children who have close contact with flea-infested cats and dogs.) These fleas consume the tapeworm eggs passed in the feces of their vertebrate host; they can act as intermediate hosts by

retaining the tapeworm larval stage, the cysticercoid, in their hemocoel until their metamorphosis to the adult form. Humans can then become infected by the inadvertent ingestion of infected fleas. A filarial nematode (*Dipetalonema reconditum*) that lives in the subcutaneous, connective, and perirenal tissues of dogs can be transmitted from host to host by *C. canis* and *C. felis*. The juvenile stage of the worm, called microfilariae, is ingested by fleas during their blood meals, develops to infective stages in the flea's fat body, migrates to the mouthparts, and then passes to the wound when the flea feeds the next time (Roberts and Janovy 2000). Fleas also may transmit *Francisella tularensis* (tularemia), *Rickettsia conori* (tick-borne typhus), *Coxiella burneti* (Q fever), *Bartonella henselae* (cat-scratch fever), and a few other minor pathogens to humans (Thomas 1996; Service 2000).

Control

For public health reasons, it is important to control fleas of rodents around our homes and on our dog and cat pets. Places that may harbor fleas within our homes, such as under carpets, floor crevices, and pet bedding materials, should be cleaned often. Various insecticidal flea powders and flea collars with slow-release vapors are effective for ridding dogs and cats of these parasites. Recently, novel, non-chemical devices such as light traps with yellow-green filters to which fleas are attracted have been shown to attract fleas from as far away as 8 m (Dryden and Broce 1993; Roberts and Janovy 2000). Finally, it is important to keep areas where livestock are maintained as free as possible from the buildup of manure, debris, and other litter.

Sucking Lice (Order Anoplura)

General

There are only about 500 described species of sucking lice and they are found only on mammals. They have small, wingless bodies that are flattened dorsoventrally. Their head, which is narrower than their prothorax, bears a pair of inconspicuous eyes. Their mouthparts consist of a flexible, sucking tube-like structure called the haustellum, which is armed on the inner surface with minute teeth; the whole structure is retracted into the head when not feeding. Because they introduce their highly modified mouthparts directly into a blood vessel when feeding, they are called true *solenophages* (Greek for pipe + eating). Several species are of considerable importance on domestic animals, and two or three species parasitize humans and can carry disease-producing microbes.

The two species of Anoplura found on humans are *Pediculus humanus* and *Phthirus pubis*. Some authorities say there are two distinct forms (subspecies) of *P. humanus*, body lice (*P. h. humanus*) and head lice (*P. h. capitis*), while others contend they are separate species, *P. capitis* and *P. humanus* (=*P. corporis*) because of subtle structural differences (Busvine 1978; Roberts and Janovy 2000; Service 2000). In either case, it is widely accepted that body lice descended from ancestral head lice after humans began to wear clothes. People who live in tropical climates often have head lice, but because they wear few clothes, body lice are usually absent. Consequently, body lice are much more prevalent in cooler, temperate regions. Although head lice stay closely associated with head hair, especially on the back of the neck and behind the ears, human body lice are unusual among Anoplura in that they spend most of their time in their host's clothing, intimately visiting their host only to take a blood meal. Both forms are highly contagious, especially under conditions of crowding and poor sanitation where people rarely wash or change their clothes. Thus, they are common in jails, refugee camps, trenches during wartime, and after disasters (wars, floods, earthquakes, etc.) where people are forced to live in unsanitary, overcrowded conditions. In the United States, elementary school children are susceptible to head lice when sharing hats, combs, and brushes.

Phthirus pubis, the "crab" louse of humans, is so-called because its middle and hind pair of legs are larger and stouter than the front pair and have massive claws that superficially resemble crabs' pincers. This species is found primarily in the pubic area, although specimens can be found amongst axillary and facial (i.e., beard, mustache, eyebrows, eyelashes) hair. It is transmitted primarily through sexual contact (Service 2000). Infestations also can arise from discarded clothing and infested bedding. Treatment involves the use of 1 percent permethrin solution available from drugstores.

Anoplura tend to be relatively host-specific, but many exceptions occur. For example, *P. humanus* also can live and breed on pigs (*Sus scrofa*), while *Haematopinus suis* of pigs readily feeds on humans. Other *Haematopinus* species infest cattle (*Bos taurus*), water buffalo (*Bubalus bubalis*), horses (*Equus caballus*), mules (*E. caballus* x *E. asinus*), and donkeys (*E. asinus*). Different *Linognathus* species parasitize cattle, sheep (*Ovis aries*), goats (*Capra hircus*), and dogs. The latter species may specialize on different regions of their host's body (e.g., legs, head), just as *Pediculus* species do on humans. Another species, *Polyplax spinulosa*, infests *Rattus*

species and transmits *Rickettsia typhi*, the causative agent of murine typhus, also carried by fleas (see above).

Development

The eggs of sucking lice, called nits, are cemented to the hair of their host, or in the case of body lice of humans, to fibers in the clothes. A female can produce up to 10 eggs per day and may produce 50-150 (head lice), 150-200 (pubic lice), or 200-300 (body lice) eggs in her life. Each egg has an operculum, or cap, at one end, usually with holes to allow the passage of air and to facilitate hatching. Lice have a hemimetabolous life cycle, meaning that the stage hatching from the egg is called a nymph, because it resembles a small adult. Depending on ambient temperature, eggs hatch in about a week, and the three nymphal stages (instars) require one to four weeks to complete their development to the adult. Nymphal stages also take blood meals, like the adults. Body lice usually do not leave their hosts voluntarily, but they are very sensitive to changes in host body temperature. Thus, they will leave their host's body when it cools after death or when the body heats due to high fever.

Diseases Carried/Caused/Transmitted

Infestation with lice is not life threatening, unless they carry disease-causing microbes. In general, the bites cause red, itching papules which may continue to exude lymph after the bite. Thus, continued scratching may lead to dermatitis and secondary bacterial infections. Years of infestation can lead to darkened, thickened areas of the skin. Allergies that produce severe itching may be caused by repeated inoculation of louse saliva when they bite. If inhaled, louse feces that are dried and become airborne may produce symptoms resembling hay fever. Human body lice can transmit three important diseases.

Louse-Borne, Endemic, or Epidemic Typhus

Typhus is caused by an obligate, intracellular bacterium *Rickettsia prowazekii*. Endemic typhus has had a significant impact on human history (see Zinsser 1934). Typhus epidemics usually coincide with anthropogenic events (war, crowding, stress, poverty, mass migrations) that favor heavy and widespread infestations of body lice; mortality during epidemics may approach 100 percent (Roberts and Janovy 2000). The disease manifests a large suite of symptoms including high fever, back- and headache, malaise, vertigo, flushed face, and petechial rashes on the armpits, flanks, chest, abdomen, back, and extremities. After about two weeks, the fever drops, profuse sweating begins, and patients become more aware of their condition. At this point, either convalescence results or increased involvement of the central nervous system begins, resulting in death. Interestingly, *R. prowazekii* is a pathogenic, often fatal parasite of the lice themselves. The rickettsial organism invades the louse's gut cells and reproduces to the point that in about 10 days the cells are destroyed, killing the louse. Before death, however, the louse's feces contain massive numbers of rickettsiae, and scratching the louse bite inoculates the organism from the feces into the bite wound. Also, the louse's strong preference for a normal body temperature stimulates it to leave the febrile patient to search for new hosts and, thus, further spreads the disease during epidemics. The rickettsial organisms also can remain infective in louse feces for up to 60 days at room temperature, and humans can become infected with typhus by inhaling dried louse feces. Humans who have survived an initial infection are important reservoir hosts because, although asymptomatic, they are still capable of infecting new lice for years. Both humans and other animal reservoirs could provide the source for new epidemics, here or elsewhere, in the event of invasions, war, famine, or other disasters (Roberts and Jaonvy 2000; Service 2000).

Trench Fever

This is a relatively uncommon and debilitating but non-fatal disease caused by another rickettsial organism, *Bartonella* (=*Rochalimaea*) *quintana*. It also is transmitted by the human body louse. The disease was first documented during World War I (1914-1918) among soldiers in trenches (thus, the name), and it reappeared again in eastern Europe during World War II (1939-1945). Scattered recent foci of infections have been documented in Bolivia and Mexico, and some cases also have been reported in the United States and Europe, mostly in homeless people (Service 2000).

Relapsing Fever

This disease of humans, also transmitted by the human body louse, is caused by a spirochete, *Borrelia recurrentis*. Spirochetes are ingested during a blood meal but only a few pass from the gut of a louse into its body cavity (haemocoel), where they reproduce and reach enormous numbers. The only way humans are infected is when the louse is crushed on the skin, releasing spirochetes to enter the body through abrasions or mucus membranes (Service 2000). Louse-borne relapsing fever apparently has disappeared from the United States (Roberts and Janovy 2000).

Control

A large variety of over-the-counter products containing insecticides effective against lice are available at most drug and grocery stores. Several, containing permethrin, are incorporated into hair care products like shampoos and cream rinses. Fine-toothed nit combs, hot water washing, machine drying, and/or dry-cleaning clothes will control human body lice. Lice on pets and domestic food animals can be controlled by insecticidal dusts and dips.

Chewing Lice (Order Mallophaga)

General

Chewing lice are wingless, dorsoventrally flattened insects with reduced (or no) eyes. There are about 3,000 named species that infest many bird and mammal species. In fact, the majority of known species are parasites of birds. None, however, have any medical significance for humans or their domesticated animals other than being significant pests. They feed primarily on hair or feathers, but some eat sebaceous secretions, mucus, and sloughed epidermal cells, while others eat the eggs and nymphs of their own species, as well as ectoparasitic mites. They also will eat blood when an irritated host scratches itself to the point of causing bleeding. Most chewing lice are only a few millimeters long and have a head that is broader than their prothorax and lack ocelli. Although many fewer species infest mammals than birds, guinea pigs (*Cavia* spp.), dogs, cats, cattle, horses, mules, asses, sheep, goats, and even Indian elephants (*Elaphas maximus*) all commonly have chewing lice on them. Irritation of the skin can become severe, especially in the young host.

Development

The development of chewing lice, from egg to adult, is similar to that seen in the Anoplura.

Diseases Carried/Caused/Transmitted

Some chewing lice can act as intermediate hosts for a number of endoparasites of mammals and birds. *Trichodectes canis*, an irritating louse of dogs that can present a severe problem to puppies, is an intermediate host for the double-pored dog tapeworm, *Dipylidium caninum*, which also can develop in people who may accidentally ingest these insects while playing with or petting their pets. The worms are transmitted when the mallophagan picks up the microfilariae by chewing on skin and eating blood from minor wounds.

Control

Mammals help control biting and other lice by grooming themselves or others. Rodents such as kangaroo rats take dust baths, which may act as a way to rid themselves of chewing lice. Other control measures are similar to those listed above for sucking lice.

Guide to Checklist Format

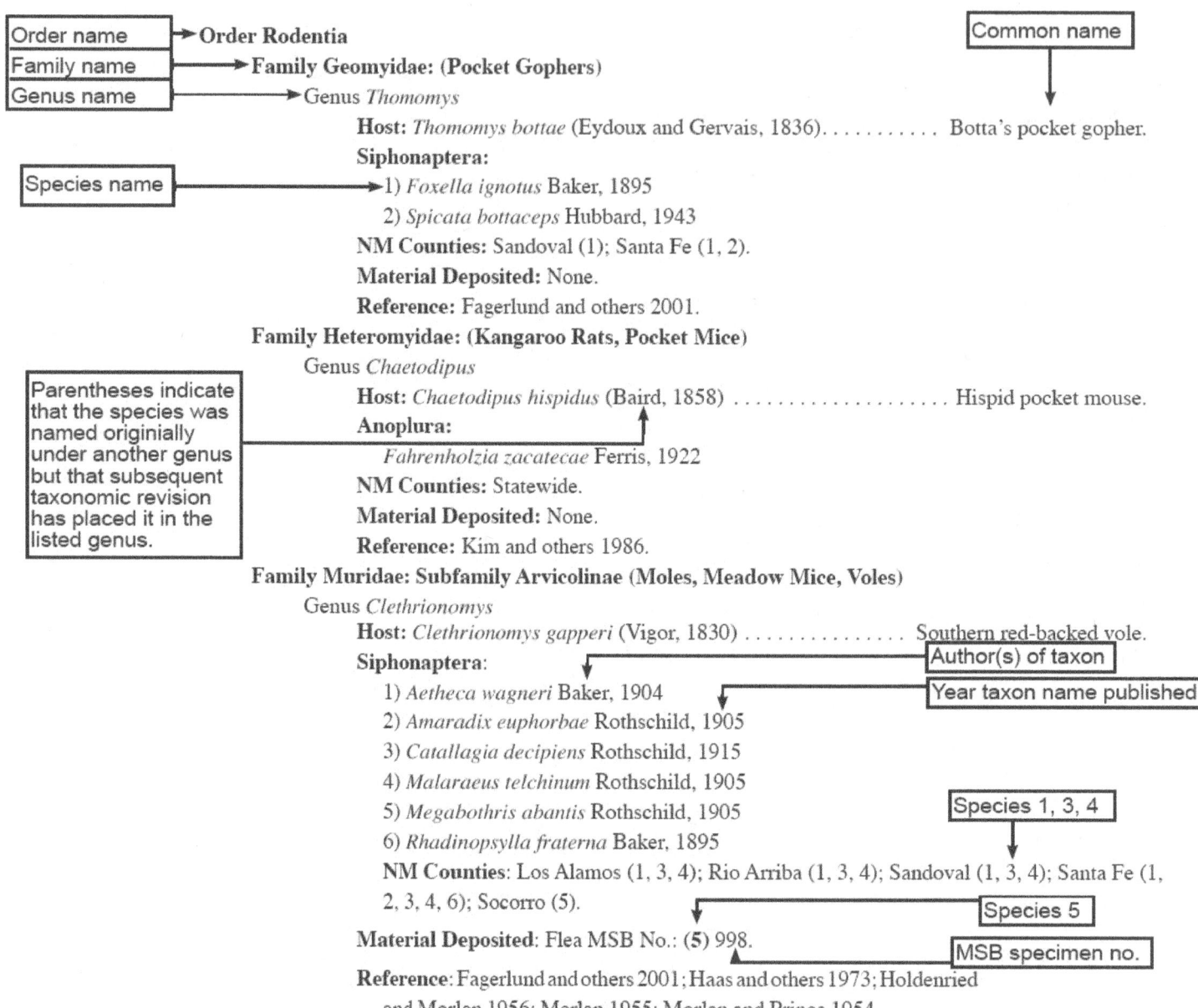

Order name → **Order Rodentia**

Family name → **Family Geomyidae: (Pocket Gophers)**

Genus name → Genus *Thomomys*

Host: *Thomomys bottae* (Eydoux and Gervais, 1836). . . . . Botta's pocket gopher.

Siphonaptera:

Species name → 1) *Foxella ignotus* Baker, 1895

2) *Spicata bottaceps* Hubbard, 1943

NM Counties: Sandoval (1); Santa Fe (1, 2).

Material Deposited: None.

Reference: Fagerlund and others 2001.

Family Heteromyidae: (Kangaroo Rats, Pocket Mice)

Genus *Chaetodipus*

Host: *Chaetodipus hispidus* (Baird, 1858) . . . . Hispid pocket mouse.

Anoplura:

Fahrenholzia zacatecae Ferris, 1922

NM Counties: Statewide.

Material Deposited: None.

Reference: Kim and others 1986.

Common name

Parentheses indicate that the species was named originially under another genus but that subsequent taxonomic revision has placed it in the listed genus.

Family Muridae: Subfamily Arvicolinae (Moles, Meadow Mice, Voles)

Genus *Clethrionomys*

Host: *Clethrionomys gapperi* (Vigor, 1830) . . . . Southern red-backed vole.

Siphonaptera:

Author(s) of taxon

1) *Aetheca wagneri* Baker, 1904

Year taxon name published

2) *Amaradix euphorbae* Rothschild, 1905

3) *Catallagia decipiens* Rothschild, 1915

4) *Malaraeus telchinum* Rothschild, 1905

5) *Megabothris abantis* Rothschild, 1905

Species 1, 3, 4

6) *Rhadinopsylla fraterna* Baker, 1895

NM Counties: Los Alamos (1, 3, 4); Rio Arriba (1, 3, 4); Sandoval (1, 3, 4); Santa Fe (1, 2, 3, 4, 6); Socorro (5).

Species 5

Material Deposited: Flea MSB No.: (**5**) 998.

MSB specimen no.

Reference: Fagerlund and others 2001; Haas and others 1973; Holdenried and Morlan 1956; Morlan 1955; Morlan and Prince 1954.

Host List—New Mexico Mammals
Class Mammalia

Order Artiodactyla

Family Cervidae: (Deer and Elk)

Genus *Odocoileus*

Host: *Odocoileus hemionus* (Rafinesque, 1817) .... Mule deer.
Siphonaptera:
    Ctenocephalides felis Bouche, 1835
NM Counties: Santa Fe.
Material Deposited: Flea MSB No.: 762.
Remarks/Observations: New state host record.
Reference: MSB Collection.

Family Bovidae: (Antelopes, Cattle, Goats, and Sheep)

Genus *Capra*

Host: *Capra hircus* Linnaeus, 1758 .... Domestic goat.
Anoplura:
    Linognathus africanus Kellogg and Paine, 1911
NM Counties: Bernalillo.
Material Deposited: None.
Reference: Kim and others 1986.

Genus *Ovis*

Host: *Ovis aries* Linnaeus, 1758 .... Mouflon.
Anoplura:
    Linognathus africanus Kellogg and Paine, 1911
NM Counties: Bernalillo.
Material Deposited: None.
Reference: Kim and others 1986.

Order Carnivora

Family Canidae: (Dogs)

Genus *Canis*

Host: *Canis familiaris* Linnaeus, 1758 .... Domestic dog.
Siphonaptera:
    1) *Euhoplopsyllus glacialis* Taschenberg, 1880
    2) *Ctenocephalides felis* Bouche, 1835
    3) *Pulex irritans* Linnaeus, 1758
    4) *Spilopsyllus inaequalis* Baker, 1895

Anoplura:

    5) *Linognathus setosus* (von Olfers, 1816)

NM Counties: Bernalillo (2, 5); Sandoval (1, 3, 4).

Material Deposited: Flea MSB No.: (**2**) 1567.

Reference: Haas and others 1973; MSB Collection.

Host: *Canis latrans* Say, 1823 . . . . Coyote.

Siphonaptera:

    1) *Euhoplopsyllus glacialis* Taschenberg, 1880

    2) *Spilopsyllus inaequalis* Baker, 1895

Anoplura:

    3) *Linognathus setosus* (von Olfers, 1816)

NM Counties: Bernalillo (3); Sandoval (1, 2).

Material Deposited: Flea MSB No.: (**1**) 859.

Reference: Haas and others 1973.

Genus *Urocyon*

Host: *Urocyon cinereoargenteus* (Schreber, 1775) . . . . Gray fox.

Siphonaptera:

    1) *Echidnophaga gallinaceus* Westwood, 1875

    2) *Euhoplopsyllus affinis* Baker, 1904

    3) *Foxella ignotus* Baker, 1895

    4) *Pulex irritans* Linnaeus, 1758

    5) *Pulex simulans* Baker, 1895

    6) *Spilopsyllus inaequalis* Baker, 1895

NM Counties: Bernalillo (1, 2, 3, 4, 5, 6); Socorro (1, 2, 3, 4, 5, 6).

Material Deposited: Flea MSB No.: (**5**) 830.

Reference: Patrick and Harrison 1995.

Genus *Vulpes*

Host: *Vulpes macrotis macrotis* Merriam, 1888. . . . . Kit fox.

Siphonaptera:

    1) *Euhoplopsyllus affinis* Baker, 1904

    2) *Foxella apachinus* C. Fox, 1914

    3) *Orchopeas agilis* Rothschild, 1905

    4) *Orchopeas caedens* Jordan, 1925

    5) *Oropsylla montanus* Baker, 1895

    6) *Pleochaetis exilis* Jordan, 1937

    7) *Pulex irritans* Linnaeus, 1758

    8) *Pulex simulans* Baker, 1895

    9) *Spilopsyllus inaequalis* Baker, 1895

    10) *Stenistomera alpina* Baker, 1895

NM Counties: Chaves (1, 3, 4, 7, 8); DeBaca (6, 7); Eddy (4); Luna (7);
McKinley (2, 4, 5, 7, 10); San Juan (8, 9); Socorro (6); Torrance (7).

Material Deposited: None.

Reference: Harrison and others 2003.

Host: *Vulpes velox velox* (Say, 1823) . . . . Swift fox.

Siphonaptera:

    1) *Echidnophaga gallinaceus* Westwood, 1875

    2) *Euhoplopsyllus affinis* Baker, 1904

    3) *Orchopeas agilis* Rothschild, 1905

    4) *Orchopeas caedens* Jordan, 1925

5) *Pulex irritans* Linnaeus, 1758

6) *Pulex simulans* Baker, 1895

NM Counties: Chaves (5, 6); Dona Ana (3); Eddy (1); Lea (2, 3, 4, 5, 6); McKinley (3); Roosevelt (5); Sandoval (3); Socorro (3); Union (5).

Material Deposited: Flea MSB No.: (**1**) 741; (**5**) 910; (**6**) 1048.

Reference: Harrison and others 2003.

Host: *Vulpes vulpes* (Linnaeus, 1758) . . . . Red fox.

Siphonaptera:

1) *Euhoplopsyllus affinis* Baker, 1904

2) *Pulex simulans* Baker, 1895

3) *Spilopsyllus inaequalis* Baker, 1895

NM Counties: McKinley (3); Roosevelt (1, 2); San Juan (2).

Material Deposited: Flea MSB No.: (**2**) 916. Lice MSB No.: None accessioned.

Reference: Harrison and others 2003.

Family Felidae: (Cats)

Genus *Felis*

Host: *Felis catus* Linnaeus, 1758. . . . . House cat.

Siphonaptera:

1) *Echidnophaga gallinaceus* Westwood, 1875

2) *Euhoplopsyllus glacialis* Taschenberg, 1880

3) *Pulex irritans* Linnaeus, 1758

4) *Spilopsyllus inaequalis* Baker, 1895

NM Counties: Bernalillo (4); Hidalgo (1); Sandoval (2, 3, 4).

Material Deposited: None.

Reference: Haas and others 1973; Jellison and Senger 1976.

Genus *Lynx*

Host: *Lynx rufus* (Schreber, 1777) . . . . Bobcat.

Siphonaptera:

1) *Euhoplopsyllus glacialis* Taschenberg, 1880

2) *Foxella ignotus* Baker, 1985

3) *Spilopsyllus inaequalis* Baker, 1895

4) *Stenistomera alpina* Baker, 1895

NM Counties: Sandoval (1, 2, 3, 4).

Material Deposited: None.

Reference: Haas and others 1973.

Family Mephitidae: (Skunks)

Genus *Mephitis*

Host: *Mephitis* sp.

Siphonaptera:

Echidnophaga gallinaceus Westwood, 1875

NM Counties: Santa Fe.

Material Deposited: Flea MSB No.: None accessioned.

Reference: Morlan 1955.

Genus *Spilogale*

Host: *Spilogale gracilis* Merriam, 1890. . . . . Western spotted skunk.

Siphonaptera:
   1) *Anomiopsyllus nudata* Baker, 1898
   2) *Hoplopsyllus anomalus* Baker, 1904
   3) *Oropsylla montanus* Baker, 1895
NM Counties: Santa Fe (1, 2, 3).
Material Deposited: None.
Reference: Morlan 1955.

Family Mustelidae: (Badgers and Weasels)

Genus *Mustela*

Host: *Mustela frenata* Lichtenstein, 1831 . . . . Long-tailed weasel.
Siphonaptera:
   1) *Foxella ignotus* Baker, 1895
   2) *Megabothris abantis* Rothschild, 1905
   3) *Thrassis pansus* Jordan, 1925
   4) *Thrassis stanfordi* Wagner, 1936
   5) *Stenistomera alpina* Baker, 1895
NM Counties: Bernalillo (1); Rio Arriba (1, 3, 4); Sandoval (2).
Material Deposited: Flea MSB No.: (**1**) 1044.
Reference: Haas and others 1973; Link 1949; Traub and Hoff 1951.

Family Procyonidae: (Raccoons and Relatives)

Genus *Bassariscus*

Host: *Bassariscus astutus* (Lichtenstein, 1830). . . . . Ringtail.
Siphonaptera:
   1) *Aetheca wagneri* Baker, 1904
   2) *Atyphloceras echis* Jordan and Rothschild, 1915
   3) *Echidnophaga gallinaceus* Westwood, 1875
   4) *Epitedia stanfordi* Traub, 1944
   5) *Malaraeus sinomus* Jordan, 1925
   6) *Megarthroglossus bisetis* Jordan and Rothschild, 1915
   7) *Meringis arachis* Jordan, 1929
   8) *Orchopeas sexdentatus neotomae* Augustson, 1943
   9) *Oropsylla montanus* Baker, 1895
   10) *Pulex simulans* Baker, 1895
   11) *Rhadinopsylla goodi* Hubbard, 1941
   12) *Stenistomera alpina* Baker, 1895
   13) *Thrassis aridis* Prince, 1944
NM Counties: Bernalillo (1, 2, 3, 4, 5, 6, 7, 8, 9, 10, 11, 12, 13); Sandoval (3).
Material Deposited: Flea MSB No.: (**3**) 1464; (**8**) 883.
Reference: Eads and others 1979, 1987; Fagerlund and others 2001;
   Haas and others 1973; Jellison and Senger 1976.

Order Chiroptera

Family Molossidae: (Molossid Bats)

Genus *Tadarida*

Host: *Tadarida brasiliensis* I. Geoffroy, 1824 . . . . Brazilian free-tailed bat.

Siphonaptera:
   Sternopsylla texanus Fox, 1914
NM Counties: Eddy.
Material Deposited: None.
Reference: Jellison and Senger 1976.

Family Vespertilionidae: (Vesper Bats)

Genus *Myotis*

Host: *Myotis thysanoides* Miller, 1897. . . . . Fringed myotis.
Siphonaptera:
   Myodopsylla nordina Traub and Hall, 1951
NM Counties: Bernalillo.
Material Deposited: None.
Reference: Traub and Hoff 1951.

Host: *Myotis yumanensis* (H. Allen, 1864) . . . . Yuma myotis.
Siphonaptera:
   Myodopsylla gentilis Jordan and Rothschild, 1921
NM Counties: Santa Fe.
Material Deposited: None.
Reference: Haas and others 1973.

Order Insectivora

Family Soricidae: (Shrews)

Genus *Sorex*

Host: *Sorex cinereus* Kerr, 1792. . . . . Cinereus shrew.
Siphonaptera:
   Corrodopsylla curvata Rothschild, 1915
NM Counties: Sandoval.
Material Deposited: Flea MSB No.: 1560.
Remarks/Observations: New state host record.
Reference: Haas and others 1973; MSB Collection.

Host: *Sorex preblei* Jackson, 1922 . . . . Preble's shrew.
Siphonaptera:
   Orchopeas agilis Rothschild, 1905
NM Counties: Sandoval.
Material Deposited: Flea MSB No.: 865.
Remarks/Observations: New state host record.
Reference: MSB Collection.

Order Lagomorpha

Family Leporidae: (Hares)

Genus *Lepus*

Host: *Lepus californicus* Gray, 1837 . . . . Black-tailed jackrabbit.

Siphonaptera:
1) *Echidnophaga gallinaceus* Westwood, 1875
2) *Euhoplopsyllus affinis* Baker, 1904
3) *Euhoplopsyllus glacialis* Taschenberg, 1880
4) *Hoplopsyllus anomalus* Baker, 1904
5) *Pleochaetis exilis* Jordan, 1937
6) *Spilopsyllus inaequalis* Baker, 1895

Anoplura:
7) *Haemodipsus setoni* Ewing, 1924

NM Counties: Bernalillo (2, 4); Chaves (3); Curry (3, 7); Dona Ana (2); Grant (1, 2); Santa Fe (2, 4, 5); Torrance (2).

Material Deposited: None.

Reference: Fagerlund and others 2001; Holdenried and Morlan 1956; Jellison and Senger 1976; Kartman 1960; Kohls 1940; Morlan 1955; Pfaffenberger and Valencia 1988; Rodriguez 1977.

Genus *Sylvilagus*

Host: *Sylvilagus audubonii* (Baird, 1858) . . . . Desert cottontail.

Siphonaptera:
1) *Aetheca wagneri* Baker, 1904
2) *Anomiopsyllus novomexicanensis* Williams and Hoff, 1951
3) *Echidnophaga gallinaceus* Westwood, 1875
4) *Euhoplopsyllus affinis* Baker, 1904
5) *Euhoplopsyllus glacialis* Taschenberg, 1880
6) *Megarthroglossus bisetis* Jordan and Rothschild, 1915
7) *Meringis bilsingi* Eads and Menzies, 1949
8) *Meringis dipodomys* Kohls, 1938
9) *Meringis nidi* Williams and Hoff, 1951
10) *Meringis rectus* Morlan, 1953
11) *Odontopsyllus dentatus* Baker, 1904
12) *Orchopeas sexdentatus* Baker, 1904
13) *Oropsylla hirsutus* Baker, 1895
14) *Polygenis gwynii* C. Fox, 1914
15) *Pulex irritans* Linnaeus, 1758
16) *Pulex simulans* Baker, 1895
17) *Rhadinopsylla fraterna* Baker, 1895
18) *Rhadinopsylla multidenticulatus* Morlan and Prince, 1954
19) *Spilopsyllus inaequalis* Baker, 1895
20) *Thrassis campestris* Prince, 1944
21) *Thrassis fotus* Jordan, 1925

Anoplura:
22) *Haemodipsus setoni* Ewing, 1924
23) *Hoplopleura hirsuta* Ferris, 1916

NM Counties: Bernalillo (9); Catron (4); Chaves (1, 2, 3, 4, 5, 6, 7, 8, 9, 10, 12, 14, 15, 16, 17, 18, 19, 20, 21); Curry (3, 5, 22); Grant (3, 4, 8, 19); Lea (3, 5); Otero (4); Rio Arriba (4, 19); Roosevelt (3, 4, 13, 16, 23); Santa Fe (1, 4, 9, 10, 11, 12, 19).

Material Deposited: Flea MSB No.: (**5**) 723; (**7**) 792; (**19**) 748.

Reference: Clark and others 1971; Eads and others 1987; Graves and others 1974; Holdenried and Morlan 1956; Kartman 1960; Kohls 1940; Link 1949; Miller and others 1970; Morlan 1955;

Pfaffenberger and Valencia 1988; Pfaffenberger and Wilson 1985; Rail and others 1969; Rodriguez 1977.

Host: *Sylvilagus floridanus* (J.A. Allen, 1890)................. Eastern cottontail.
Siphonaptera:
    1) *Euhoplopsyllus affinis* Baker, 1904
NM Counties: Sandoval.
Material Deposited: Flea MSB No.: 749.
Reference: MSB Collection.

Host: *Sylvilagus nuttalli* (Bachman, 1837) .... Mountain cottontail.
Siphonaptera:
    1) *Euhoplopsyllus affinis* Baker, 1904
    2) *Megarthroglossus bisetis* Jordan and Rothschild, 1915
    3) *Odontopsyllus dentatus* Baker, 1904
    4) *Spilopsyllus inaequalis* Baker, 1895
    5) *Stenistomera alpina* Baker, 1895
NM Counties: Rio Arriba (1, 4); Sandoval (1, 2, 3, 5).
Material Deposited: None.
Reference: Haas and others 1973; Link 1949; Mendez and Haas 1973.

Host: *Sylvilagus* sp.
Siphonaptera:
    1) *Anomiopsyllus novomexicanensis* Williams and Hoff, 1951
    2) *Echidnophaga gallinaceus* Westwood, 1875
    3) *Euhoplopsyllus affinis* Baker, 1904
    4) *Eumolpianus eumolpi* Rothschild, 1905
    5) *Hoplopsyllus anomalus* Baker, 1904
    6) *Megarthroglossus bisetis* Jordan and Rothschild, 1915
    7) *Meringis bilsingi* Eads and Menzies, 1949
    8) *Meringis dipodomys* Kohls, 1938
    9) *Meringis nidi* Williams and Hoff, 1951
    10) *Meringis rectus* Morlan, 1953
    11) *Oropsylla montanus* Baker, 1895
    12) *Polygenis gwyni* Fox, 1914
    13) *Pulex irritans* Linnaeus, 1758
    14) *Rhadinopsylla fraterna* Baker, 1895
    15) *Thrassis fotus* Jordan, 1925
NM Counties: Bernalillo (3, 4, 5); Chaves (1, 2, 3, 6, 7, 8, 9, 10, 12, 13, 14, 15); Sandoval (11).
Material Deposited: None.
Reference: Forcum and others 1969; Jellison and Senger 1976; Kohls 1940.

Family Ochotonidae: (Pikas)

Genus *Ochotona*

Host: *Ochotona princeps* (Richardson, 1828) .... American pika.
Siphonaptera:
    1) *Amphalius necopinus* Jordan, 1925
    2) *Ctenophyllus armatus* Wagner, 1901
    3) *Megabothris abantis* Rothschild, 1905
    4) *Megarthroglossus bisetis* Jordan and Rothschild, 1915

5) *Megarthroglossus divisus* Baker, 1898
6) *Phalacropsylla morlani* Eads and Campos, 1982
7) *Spilopsyllus inaequalis* Baker, 1895
8) *Stenistomera alpina* Baker, 1895
NM Counties: Sandoval (4, 8); Santa Fe (1, 2, 3, 5, 6, 7, 8).
Material Deposited: None.
Reference: Haas and others 1973; Holdenried and Morlan 1956; Mendez and Haas 1973; Morlan 1955.

Order Perissodactyla

Family Equidae: (Equine)

Genus *Equus*

Host: *Equus asinus* Linnaeus, 1758 . . . . Ass.
Anoplura;
   1) *Haematopinus asini* Linnaeus, 1758
Mallophaga:
   2) *Werneckiella (Bovicola) equi* (Denny, 1842)
NM Counties: Otero (1, 2).
Material Deposited: None.
Reference: Kim and others 1986.

Host: *Equus caballus* Linnaeus, 1758 . . . . Horse.
Anoplura:
   1) *Haematopinus asini* Linnaeus, 1758
Mallophaga:
   2) *Werneckiella (Bovicola) equi* (Denny, 1842)
NM Counties: Otero (1, 2).
Material Deposited: None.
Reference: Kim and others 1986.

Order Primates

Family Hominidae: (Humans)

Genus *Homo*

Host: *Homo sapiens* Linnaeus, 1758 . . . . Human.
Siphonaptera:
   1) *Pulex irritans*
Anoplura:
   2) *Pediculus humanus* Linnaeus, 1758
   3) *Phthirus pubis* (Linnaeus, 1758)
NM Counties: Bernalillo (2, 3); Los Alamos (1); Rio Arriba (1); Sandoval (1); Santa Fe (1).
Material Deposited: None.
Reference: MSB Collection.

Order Rodentia

Family Geomyidae: (Pocket Gophers)

Genus *Thomomys*

Host: *Thomomys bottae* (Eydoux and Gervais, 1836) . . . . Botta's pocket gopher.
Siphonaptera:
  1) *Foxella ignotus* Baker, 1895
  2) *Spicata bottaceps* Hubbard, 1943
NM Counties: Sandoval (1); Santa Fe (1, 2).
Material Deposited: None.
Reference: Fagerlund and others 2001; Haas and others 1973; Holdenried and Morlan 1956; Morlan 1955.

Host: *Thomomys talpoides* (Richardson, 1828) . . . . Northern pocket gopher.
Siphonaptera:
  1) *Anomiopsyllus nudata* Baker, 1898
  2) *Ctenophyllus armatus* Wagner, 1901
  3) *Dactylopsylla neomexicana* Prince, 1945
  4) *Eumolpianus eumolpi* Rothschild, 1905
  5) *Foxella ignotus* Baker, 1895
  6) *Megarthroglossus bisetis* Jordan and Rothschild, 1915
  7) *Spicata rara* Fox, 1940
NM Counties: San Miguel (3); Sandoval (5, 7); Santa Fe (1, 2, 4, 5, 6).
Material Deposited: None.
Reference: Haas 1973; Haas and others 1973; Holdenried and Morlan 1956; Morlan 1955; Prince 1945.

Family Heteromyidae: (Kangaroo Rats, Pocket Mice)

Genus *Chaetodipus*

Host: *Chaetodipus hispidus* (Baird, 1858) . . . . Hispid pocket mouse.
Anoplura:
  Fahrenholzia zacatecae Ferris, 1922
NM Counties: Statewide.
Material Deposited: None.
Reference: Kim and others 1986.

Host: *Chaetodipus intermedius* Merriam, 1889 . . . . Rock pocket mouse.
Anoplura:
  Fahrenholzia pinnata Kellogg and Ferris, 1915
NM Counties: Bernalillo, Luna, Otero, Roosevelt, Santa Fe, Socorro.
Material Deposited: None.
Reference: Kim and others 1986; Morlan and Hoff 1957; Pfaffenberger and deBruin 1986.

Genus *Dipodomys*

Host: *Dipodomys merriami* Mearns, 1890 . . . . Merriam's kangaroo rat.
Siphonaptera:
  1) *Aetheca wagneri* Baker, 1904
  2) *Anomiopsyllus novomexicanensis* Williams and Hoff, 1951

3) *Anomiopsyllus hiemalis mexicanus* Holland, 1965
4) *Echidnophaga gallinaceus* Westwood, 1875
5) *Euhoplopsyllus affinis* Taschenberg, 1880
6) *Eumolpianus eumolpi* Rothschild, 1905
7) *Meringis altipecten* Traub and Hoff, 1951
8) *Meringis arachis* Jordan, 1929
9) *Meringis bilsingi* Eads and Menzies, 1949
10) *Meringis dipodomys* Kohls, 1938
11) *Meringis disparilis* Eads, 1979
12) *Meringis nidi* Williams and Hoff, 1951
13) *Meringis parkeri* Jordan, 1937
14) *Meringis rectus* Morlan, 1953
15) *Orchopeas leucopus* Baker, 1904
16) *Oropsylla montanus* Baker, 1895
17) *Rhadinopsylla fraterna* Baker, 1895
18) *Rhadinopsylla multidenticulatus* Morlan and Prince, 1954
19) *Thrassis campestris* Prince, 1944
20) *Thrassis fotus* Jordan, 1925

Anoplura:
21) *Fahrenholzia pinnata* Kellogg and Ferris, 1915
22) *Haematopinus asini* Linnaeus, 1758

NM Counties: Chaves (2, 4, 5, 9, 10, 12, 14, 17, 18, 19, 20); Colfax (3); Dona Ana (7, 11); Eddy (11, 12); Hidalgo (8, 12); Luna (7, 11, 21); Otero (9, 12, 14, 21, 22); Rio Arriba (1, 13); Santa Fe (15); Sierra (9, 13); Socorro (5, 6, 15, 16); Valencia (2).

Material Deposited: Flea MSB No.: (**2**) 794; (**4**) 714; (**6**) 724; (**7**) 1060; (**8**) 940; (**9**) 992; (**10**) 1028; (**12**) 1003; (**13**) 956; (**15**) 838; (**16**) 1011; (**19**) 875.

Reference: Barnes and others 1977; Eads 1978; Eads and others 1987; Graves and others 1974; Kim and others 1986; Link 1949; Miller and others 1970; Rail and others 1969; Traub and Hoff 1951.

Host: *Dipodomys ordii* Woodhouse, 1853 . . . . Ord's kangaroo rat.
Siphonaptera:
1) *Aetheca wagneri* Baker, 1904
2) *Anomiopsyllus novomexicanensis* Williams and Hoff, 1951
3) *Echidnophaga gallinaceus* Westwood, 1875
4) *Malaraeus sinomus* Jordan, 1925
5) *Meringis altipecten* Traub and Hoff, 1951
6) *Meringis arachis* Jordan, 1929
7) *Meringis bilsingi* Eads and Menzies, 1949
8) *Meringis dipodomys* Kohls, 1938
9) *Meringis disparilis* Eads, 1979
10) *Merinigs facilis* Eads, 1979
11) *Meringis nidi* Williams and Hoff, 1951
12) *Meringis parkeri* Jordan, 1937
13) *Meringis rectus* Morlan, 1953
14) *Orchopeas leucopus* Baker, 1904
15) *Peromyscopsylla adelpha* Rothschild, 1915
16) *Pleochaetis exilis* Jordan, 1937
17) *Rhadinopsylla multidenticulatus* Morlan and Prince, 1954
18) *Thrassis aridis* Prince, 1944

19) *Thrassis bacchi consimilis* Stark, 1957
20) *Thrassis campestris* Prince, 1944
21) *Thrassis fotus* Jordan, 1925
22) *Thrassis pansus* Jordan, 1925

Anoplura:

23) *Fahrenholzia pinnata* Kellogg and Ferris, 1915
24) *Hoplopleura arboricola* Kellogg and Ferris, 1915
25) *Hoplopleura ferrisi* Cook and Beer, 1959
26) *Hoplopleura hesperomydis* (Osborn, 1891)
27) *Hoplopleura hirsuta* Ferris, 1916
29) *Neohaematopinus neotomae* Ferris, 1941
30) *Polyplax auricularis* Kellogg and Ferris, 1915

Mallophaga:

31) *Goniodes squamatus* Emerson, 1950

NM Counties: Bernalillo (7, 31); Catron (12); Chaves (3, 7, 8, 10, 11, 13, 20); Dona Ana (2, 9); Grant (6); Hidalgo (18); Lea (8, 11, 12, 21); Luna (2, 7, 9); Roosevelt (7, 16, 18, 23, 27, 30); Sandoval (8, 12); Santa Fe (1, 11, 12, 13, 14, 15, 16, 17, 20, 22); Sierra (5, 6); Socorro (4); Torrance (13).

Material Deposited: Flea MSB No.: (**3**) 732; (**4**) 1027; (**5**) 957; (**11**) 1004; (**12**) 928; (**18**) 844; (**19**) 898.

Reference: Barnes and others 1977; Eads 1978; Eads and others 1987; Fagerlund and others 2001; Graves and others 1974; Haas and others 1973; Holdenried and Morlan 1956; Jellison and Senger 1976; Kartman 1960; Kim 1965; Kim and others 1986; Miller and others 1970; Morlan 1955; Morlan and Prince 1954; Pfaffenberger and deBruin 1986; Prince 1944; Rail and others 1969; Williams and Hoff 1951.

Host: *Dipodomys spectabilis* Merriam, 1890. . . . . Banner-tailed kangaroo rat.

Siphonaptera:

1) *Anomiopsyllus novomexicanensis* Williams and Hoff, 1951
2) *Echidnophaga gallinaceus* Westwood, 1875
3) *Euhoplopsyllus affinis* Taschenberg, 1880
4) *Megarthroglossus bisetis* Jordan and Rothschild, 1915
5) *Meringis altipecten* Traub and Hoff, 1951
6) *Meringis arachis* Jordan, 1929
7) *Meringis bilsingi* Eads and Menzies, 1949
8) *Meringis dipodomys* Kohls, 1938
9) *Meringis jamesoni* Hubbard, 1943
10) *Meringis nidi* Williams and Hoff, 1951
11) *Meringis parkeri* Jordan, 1937
12) *Meringis rectus* Morlan, 1953
13) *Orchopeas sexdentatus* Baker, 1904
14) *Pleochaetis exilis* Jordan, 1937
15) *Polygenis gwynii* C. Fox, 1914
16) *Pulex irritans* Linnaeus, 1758
17) *Pulex simulans* Baker, 1895
18) *Rhadinopsylla fraterna* Baker, 1895
19) *Rhadinopsylla multidenticulatus* Morlan and Prince, 1954
20) *Thrassis campestris* Prince, 1944
21) *Thrassis fotus* Jordan, 1925
22) *Thrassis pansus* Jordan, 1925

Anoplura:

    23) *Fahrenholzia pinnata* Kellogg and Ferris, 1915

    24) *Hoplopleura acanthopus* (Burmeister, 1839)

    25) *Hoplopleura arboricola* Kellogg and Ferris, 1915

NM Counties: Bernalillo (10, 12, 25); Chaves (1, 2, 3, 4, 7, 8, 10, 12, 15, 16, 17, 18, 19, 20, 21); Dona Ana (6, 12); Lincoln (12); Luna (5, 6, 23); San Juan (12); Sandoval (12); Santa Fe (3, 6, 9, 10, 11, 12, 13, 19, 20, 22, 23, 24, 25); Sierra (6); Socorro (6); Valencia (12).

Material Deposited: Flea MSB No.: (**2**) 718; (**5**) 944; (**6**) 926; (**8**) 951; (**10**) 938.

Reference: Clark and others 1971; Eads and others 1987; Fagerlund and others 2001; Graves and others 1974; Holdenried and Morlan 1955, 1956; Jellison and Senger 1976; Kim and others 1986; Miller and others 1970; Morlan 1955; Morlan and Prince 1954; Rail and others 1969; Traub and Hoff 1951; Williams and Hoff 1951.

Genus *Perognathus*

Host: *Perognathus flavescens* Merriam, 1889 . . . . Plains pocket mouse.

Siphonaptera:

    1) *Meringis arachis* Jordan, 1929

    2) *Thrassis pansus* Jordan, 1925

NM Counties: Socorro (1, 2).

Material Deposited: Flea MSB No.: (**1**) 939; (**3**) 879.

Reference: MSB Collection.

Host: *Perognathus flavus* Baird, 1855 . . . . Silky pocket mouse.

Siphonaptera:

    1) *Anomiopsyllus nudata* Baker, 1898

    2) *Epitedia stanfordi* Traub, 1944

    3) *Euhoplopsyllus affinis* Baker, 1904

    4) *Meringis arachis* Jordan, 1929

    5) *Meringis dipodomys* Eads, 1979

    6) *Meringis facilis* Eads, 1979

    7) *Meringis jamesoni* Hubbard, 1943

    8) *Meringis nidi* Williams and Hoff, 1951

    9) *Meringis parkeri* Jordan, 1937

    10) *Meringis rectus* Morlan, 1953

    11) *Orchopeas leucopus* Baker, 1904

    12) *Oropsylla idahoensis* Baker, 1904

Anoplura:

    13) *Fahrenholzia pinnata* Kellogg and Ferris, 1915

NM Counties: Chaves (5, 6, 10); Santa Fe (1, 2, 3, 7, 8, 9, 10, 11, 12, 13); Socorro (4, 12); Union (7).

Material Deposited: Flea MSB No.: (**4**) 1000; (**8**) 931; (**12**) 1007.

Reference: Eads 1978; Eads and others 1987; Fagerlund and others 2001; Graves and others 1974; Haas and others 1973; Holdenried and Morlan 1956; Kim and others 1986; Morlan 1955; Rail and others 1969.

Family Muridae: Subfamily Arvicolinae (Moles, Meadow Mice, Voles)

Genus *Clethrionomys*

Host: *Clethrionomys gapperi* (Vigor, 1830). . . . . Southern red-backed vole.

Siphonaptera:
1) *Aetheca wagneri* Baker, 1904
2) *Amaradix euphorbae* Rothschild, 1905
3) *Catallagia decipiens* Rothschild, 1915
4) *Malaraeus telchinum* Rothschild, 1905
5) *Megabothris abantis* Rothschild, 1905
6) *Rhadinopsylla fraterna* Baker, 1895

NM Counties: Los Alamos (1, 3, 4); Rio Arriba (1, 3, 4); Sandoval (1, 3, 4); Santa Fe (1, 2, 3, 4, 6); Socorro (5).

Material Deposited: Flea MSB No.: (**5**) 998.

Reference: Fagerlund and others 2001; Haas and others 1973; Holdenried and Morlan 1956; Morlan 1955; Morlan and Prince 1954.

Genus *Microtus*

Host: *Microtus longicaudus* (Merriam, 1888) . . . . Long-tailed vole.
Siphonaptera:
1) *Aetheca wagneri* Baker, 1904
2) *Catallagia decipiens* Rothschild, 1915
3) *Delotelis telegoni* Rothschild, 1905
4) *Eumolpianus eumolpi americanus* Hubbard, 1950
5) *Hystrichopsylla dippiei* Rothschild, 1902
6) *Malaraeus telchinum* Rothschild, 1905
7) *Megabothris abantis* Rothschild, 1905
8) *Megarthroglossus bisetis* Jordan and Rothschild, 1915
9) *Oropsylla idahoensis* Baker, 1904
10) *Peromyscopsylla adelpha* Rothschild, 1915
11) *Peromyscopsylla hamifer vigens* Jordan, 1837
12) *Peromyscopsylla selenis* Rothschild, 1906

Anoplura:
13) *Hoplopleura acanthopus* (Burmeister, 1839)
14) *Hoplopleura hesperomydis* (Osborn, 1891)

NM Counties: Sandoval (1, 2, 5, 6, 7, 8, 9, 10, 11); Santa Fe (1, 2, 3, 4, 5, 6, 7, 11, 12, 13, 14).

Material Deposited: None.

Reference: Fagerlund and others 2001; Haas 1973; Haas and others 1973; Holdenried and Morlan 1956; Kim and others 1986; Mendez and Haas 1973; Morlan 1955.

Host: *Microtus mexicanus* (Saussure, 1861) . . . . Mexican vole.
Siphonaptera:
1) *Ctenophthalmus pseudagyrtes* Baker, 1904
2) *Hystrichopsylla dippiei* Rothschild, 1902
3) *Plusaetis equatorius asetus* Traub, 1950

NM Counties: Socorro (1, 2, 3).

Material Deposited: Flea MSB No.: (**1**) 743; (**2**) 1017; (**3**) 947.

Reference: Fagerlund and others 2001; MSB Collection.

Host: *Microtus montanus* (Peale, 1848). . . . . Montane vole.
Siphonaptera:
1) *Aetheca wagneri* Baker, 1904
2) *Catallagia decipiens* Rothschild, 1915

3) *Corrodopsylla curvata* Rothschild, 1915
4) *Dactylopsylla bluei* Fox, 1909
5) *Foxella ignotus* Baker, 1895
6) *Hystrichopsylla dippiei* Rothschild, 1902
7) *Malaraeus telchinum* Rothschild, 1905
8) *Megabothris abantis* Rothschild, 1905
9) *Peromyscopsylla hamifer vigens* Jordan, 1937
10) *Peromyscopsylla selenis* Rothschild, 1906
11) *Spicata rara* Fox, 1940

NM Counties: San Miguel (4); Sandoval (1, 2, 3, 5, 6, 7, 8, 9, 10, 11).
Material Deposited: None.
Reference: Fagerlund and others 2001; Haas 1973; Haas and others 1973.

Host: *Microtus pennsylvanicus* (Ord, 1815). . . . . Meadow vole.
Siphonaptera:
1) *Megabothris megacolpus* Jordan, 1929
2) *Peromyscopsylla hamifer vigens* Jordan, 1937
3) *Peromyscopsylla selenis* Rothschild, 1906

NM Counties: Colfax (1); San Miguel (2, 3); Sandoval (2, 3).
Material Deposited: None.
Reference: Johnson and Traub 1954.

Host: *Microtus* sp.
Siphonaptera:
1) *Catallagia decipiens* Rothschild, 1915
2) *Megabothris abantis* Rothschild, 1905
3) *Meringis parkeri* Jordan, 1937
4) *Eumolpianus eumolpi* Rothschild, 1905

NM Counties: Rio Arriba (1, 2, 3, 4).
Material Deposited: None.
Reference: Link 1949.

Subfamily Murinae: (Old World Rats and Mice)

Genus *Mus*

Host: *Mus musculus* Linnaeus, 1758 . . . . House mouse.
Siphonaptera:
    Aetheca wagneri Baker, 1904
NM Counties: Sandoval.
Material Deposited: None.
Reference: Fagerlund and others 2001; Haas and others 1973.

Genus *Rattus*

Host: *Rattus norvegicus* (Berkenhout, 1769). . . . . Brown rat.
Siphonaptera:
1) *Echidnophaga gallinaceus* Westwood, 1875
2) *Nosophyllus fasciatus* Bosc, 1800
3) *Xenopsylla cheopis* Rothschild, 1903

NM Counties: Bernalillo (1, 2, 3); Chaves (1); Hidalgo (3); Valencia (2).
Material Deposited: None.
Reference: Becker 1947; Prince 1943.

Host: *Rattus rattus* (Linnaeus, 1758) . . . . House rat.
Siphonaptera:
    Xenopsylla cheopis Rothschild, 1903
NM Counties: Hidalgo.
Material Deposited: None.
Reference: Becker 1947; Prince 1943.

Subfamily Sigmodontinae: (New World Rats and Mice)

Genus *Neotoma*

Host: *Neotoma albigula* Hartley, 1894. . . . . White-throated woodrat.
Siphonaptera:
    1) *Aetheca wagneri* Baker, 1904
    2) *Anomiopsyllus hiemalis* Eads and Menzies, 1948
    3) *Anomiopsyllus hiemalis mexicanus* Holland, 1965
    4) *Anomiopsyllus novomexicanensis* Williams and Hoff, 1951
    5) *Anomiopsyllus nudata* Baker, 1898
    6) *Atyphloceras echis* Jordan and Rothschild, 1915
    7) *Echidnophaga gallinaceus* Westwood, 1875
    8) *Epitedia stanfordi* Traub, 1944
    9) *Hoplopsyllus anomalus* Baker, 1904
    10) *Malaraeus sinomus* Jordan, 1925
    11) *Megarthroglossus bisetis* Jordan and Rothschild, 1915
    12) *Megarthroglossus divisus* Baker, 1898
    13) *Megarthroglossus procus* Jordan and Rothschild, 1915
    14) *Meringis altipecten* Traub and Hoff, 1951
    15) *Meringis arachis* Jordan, 1929
    16) *Meringis jamesoni* Hubbard, 1943
    17) *Meringis nidi* Williams and Hoff, 1951
    18) *Meringis parkeri* Jordan, 1937
    19) *Meringis rectus* Morlan, 1953
    20) *Orchopeas agilis* Rothschild, 1905
    21) *Orchopeas leucopus* Baker, 1904
    22) *Orchopeas sexdentatus* Baker, 1904
    23) *Orchopeas sexdentatus neotomae* Auguston, 1943
    24) *Oropsylla montanus* Baker, 1895
    25) *Peromyscopsylla hesperomys* Baker, 1904
    26) *Phalacropsylla hamata* Tipton and Mendez, 1968
    27) *Pleochaetis exilis* Jordan, 1937
    28) *Rhadinopsylla multidenticulatus* Morlan and Prince, 1954
    29) *Rhadinopsylla sectilis* Jordan and Rothschild, 1923
    30) *Stenistomera alpina* Baker, 1895
    31) *Stenistomera macrodactyla* Good, 1942
    32) *Thrassis bacchi consimilis* Stark, 1957
    33) *Thrassis campestris* Prince, 1944
    34) *Thrassis pansus* Jordan, 1925
Anoplura:
    35) *Neohaematopinus neotomae* Ferris, 1941
NM Counties: Bernalillo (3, 4, 11, 12, 22, 25, 26, 30, 35); Catron (3);
    Chaves (2); Colfax (3); Dona Ana (4, 14, 17, 20); Eddy (2, 14); Grant
    (6); Guadalupe (11); Hidalgo (4, 14, 15); Lea (2, 7, 22); Lincoln (3,
    4, 12); Luna (4); McKinley (20); Otero (4, 12); Rio Arriba (1, 4, 7,

22, 23); San Juan (4); Sandoval (11, 13, 29); Santa Fe (1, 3, 5, 6, 7, 8, 9, 10, 11, 12, 16, 17, 18, 19, 21, 22, 23, 24, 28, 30, 31, 33, 34, 35); Sierra (4); Socorro (3, 4, 18, 20, 32); Valencia (4).

Material Deposited: Flea MSB No.: (**3**) 701; (**4**) 702; (**5**) 758; (**7**) 720; (**12**) 1008; (**13**) 1006; (**15**) 977; (**20**) 784; (**21**) 771; (**23**) 971; (**32**) 884.

Reference: Barnes and others 1977; Eads and Campos 1982; Eads and others 1987; Fagerlund and others 2001; Good 1942; Haas and others 1973; Holdenried and Morlan 1955, 1956; Kartman 1960; Kim and others 1986; Link 1949; Mendez 1956; Mendez and Haas 1973; Morlan 1955; Morlan and Prince 1954; Tipton and others 1979; Traub and Hoff 1951.

Host: *Neotoma cinerea* (Ord, 1815) . . . . Bushy-tailed woodrat.
Siphonaptera:
1) *Aetheca wagneri* Baker, 1904
2) *Amaradix vonfintelis* Prince, 1959
3) *Catallagia decipiens* Rothschild, 1915
4) *Hystrichopsylla dippiei* Rothschild, 1902
5) *Malaraeus telchinum* Rothschild, 1905
6) *Megarthroglossus bisetis* Jordan and Rothschild, 1915
7) *Megarthroglossus cavernicolus* Mendez and Haas, 1972
8) *Megarthroglossus divisus* Baker, 1898
9) *Orchopeas sexdentatus* Baker, 1904
10) *Orchopeas sexdentatus neotomae* Auguston, 1943
11) *Phalacropsylla allos* Wagner, 1936
12) *Rhadinopsylla fraterna* Baker, 1895
13) *Rhadinopsylla sectilis* Jordan and Rothschild, 1923
14) *Stenistomera alpina* Baker, 1895

NM Counties: Colfax (6, 8); McKinley (6); Rio Arriba (9); Sandoval (1, 2, 3, 5, 6, 7, 9, 10, 11, 12, 13, 14); Santa Fe (1, 3, 4, 9, 10, 14).

Material Deposited: Flea MSB No.: (**14**) 814.

Reference: Eads and others 1987; Haas and others 1973; Holdenried and Morlan 1956; Link 1949; Mendez 1956; Mendez and Haas 1973; Morlan 1955; Tipton and others 1979.

Host: *Neotoma lepida* Thomas, 1893 . . . . Desert wood rat.
Siphonaptera:
Anomiopsyllus novomexicanensis Williams and Hoff, 1951
NM Counties: Hidalgo.
Material Deposited: None.
Reference: Barnes and others 1977.

Host: *Neotoma mexicana* Baird, 1855 . . . . Mexican woodrat.
Siphonaptera:
1) *Aetheca wagneri* Baker, 1904
2) *Amaradix vonfintelis* Prince, 1959
3) *Anomiopsyllus hiemalis mexicanus* Holland, 1965
4) *Anomiopsyllus novomexicanensis* Williams and Hoff, 1951
5) *Anomiopsyllus nudata* Baker, 1898
6) *Catallagia decipiens* Rothschild, 1915
7) *Eumolpianus eumolpi* Rothschild, 1905
8) *Hystrichopsylla dippiei* Rothschild, 1902

9) *Malaraeus sinomus* Jordan, 1925

10) *Malaraeus telchinum* Rothschild, 1905

11) *Megabothris abantis* Rothschild, 1905

12) *Megarthroglossus bisetis* Jordan and Rothschild, 1915

13) *Orchopeas sexdentatus* Baker, 1904

14) *Orchopeas sexdentatus neotomae* Auguston, 1943

15) *Phalacropsylla allos* Wagner, 1936

16) *Pleochaetis exilis* Jordan, 1937

17) *Stenistomera alpina* Baker, 1895

Anoplura:

18) *Neohaematopinus neotomae* Ferris, 1941

NM Counties: Bernalillo (14, 18); Catron (3); McKinley (12); Rio Arriba (4); Sandoval (1, 2, 6, 8, 10, 11, 12, 13, 14, 15, 17); Santa Fe (5, 7, 9, 13, 14, 16, 17, 18); Taos (3).

Material Deposited: None.

Reference: Barnes and others 1977; Haas and others 1973; Holdenried and Morlan 1956; Kim and others 1986; Link 1949; Mendez and Haas 1973; Morlan 1955; Tipton and others 1979; Traub and Hoff 1951.

Host: *Neotoma micropus* Baird, 1855 . . . . Southern plains woodrat.

Siphonaptera:

1) *Aetheca wagneri* Baker, 1904

2) *Anomiopsyllus novomexicanensis* Williams and Hoff, 1951

3) *Anomiopsyllus nudata* Baker, 1898

4) *Atyphloceras echis* Jordan and Rothschild, 1915

5) *Echidnophaga gallinaceus* Westwood, 1875

6) *Epitedia stanfordi* Traub, 1944

7) *Megarthroglossus bisetis* Jordan and Rothschild, 1915

8) *Megarthroglossus divisus* Baker, 1898

9) *Meringis bilsingi* Eads and Menzies, 1949

10) *Meringis dipodomys* Kohls, 1938

11) *Meringis facilis* Eads, 1979

12) *Meringis nidi* Williams and Hoff, 1951

13) *Meringis parkeri* Jordan, 1937

14) *Meringis rectus* Morlan, 1953

15) *Orchopeas leucopus* Baker, 1904

16) *Orchopeas sexdentatus* Baker, 1904

17) *Orchopeas sexdentatus neotomae* Auguston, 1943

18) *Peromyscopsylla draco* Hopkins, 1951

19) *Pleochaetis exilis* Jordan, 1937

20) *Polygenis gwynii* (C. Fox, 1914)

21) *Rhadinopsylla multidenticulatus* Morlan and Prince, 1954

22) *Thrassis campestris* Prince, 1944

23) *Thrassis fotus* Jordan, 1925

24) *Thrassis pansus* Jordan, 1925

Anoplura:

25) *Neohaematopinus neotomae* Ferris, 1941

NM Counties: Bernalillo (2, 4, 6, 7, 13, 16); Chaves (1, 2, 5, 7, 9, 10, 11, 12, 14, 16, 20, 21, 22, 23); Santa Fe (1, 3, 6, 7, 8, 12, 13, 14, 15, 16, 17, 18, 19, 21, 22, 24).

Material Deposited: None.

Reference: Graves and others 1974; Holdenried and Morlan 1956; Jellison and Senger 1976; Kim and others 1986; Miller and others 1970; Morlan 1955; Morlan and Prince 1954; Williams and Hoff 1951.

Host: *Neotoma* sp.
Siphonaptera:
1) *Anomiopsyllus novomexicanensis* Williams and Hoff, 1951
2) *Anomiopsyllus hiemalis mexicanus* Holland, 1965
3) *Atyphloceras echis* Jordan and Rothschild, 1915
4) *Echidnophaga gallinaceus* Westwood, 1875
5) *Euhoplopsyllus affinis* Baker, 1904
6) *Malaraeus telchinum* Rothschild, 1905
7) *Megarthroglossus bisetis* Jordan and Rothschild, 1915
8) *Meringis bilsingi* Eads and Menzies, 1949
9) *Meringis dipodomys* Kohls, 1938
10) *Meringis nidi* Williams and Hoff, 1951
11) *Meringis rectus* Morlan, 1953
12) *Orchopeas leucopus* Baker, 1904
13) *Orchopeas sexdentatus* Baker, 1904
14) *Polygenis gwynii* C. Fox, 1914
15) *Rhadinopsylla fraterna* Baker, 1895
16) *Thrassis campestris* Prince, 1944
17) *Thrassis fotus* Jordan, 1925
Anoplura:
18) *Linognathoides neotomae* Ferris, 1942
NM Counties: Bernalillo (1, 3, 7, 18); Chaves (1, 3, 4, 5, 6, 7, 8, 9, 10, 11, 12, 13, 14, 15, 16, 17); Colfax (2); Otero (18); Lea (13); San Miguel (7); Santa Fe (7, 18); Valencia (2).
Material Deposited: None.
Reference: Barnes and others 1977; Jellison and Senger 1976; Jordan and Rothschild 1915; Kartman 1960; Kim and others 1986; Mendez 1956; Morlan 1955; Rail and others 1969.

Genus *Onychomys*

Host: *Onychomys arenicola* Mearns, 1896 . . . . Mearn's grasshopper mouse.
Siphonaptera:
1) *Meringis altipecten* Traub and Hoff, 1951
2) *Orchopeas caedens* Jordan, 1925
NM Counties: Socorro (1, 2).
Material Deposited: Flea MSB No.: (**1**) 967; (**2**) 870.
Reference: MSB Collection.

Host: *Onychomys leucogaster* (Wied-Neuwied, 1841) . . . Northern grasshopper mouse.
Siphonaptera:
1) *Aetheca wagneri* Baker, 1904
2) *Anomiopsyllus novomexicanensis* Williams and Hoff, 1951
3) *Echidnophaga gallinaceus* Westwood, 1875
4) *Epitedia stanfordi* Traub, 1944
5) *Malaraeus sinomus* Jordan, 1925
6) *Malaraeus telchinum* Rothschild, 1905
7) *Megarthroglossus bisetis* Jordan and Rothschild, 1915
8) *Megarthroglossus divisus* Baker, 1898

9) *Meringis altipecten* Traub and Hoff, 1951
10) *Meringis arachis* (Jordan, 1929)
11) *Meringis bilsingi* Eads and Menzies, 1949
12) *Meringis dipodomys* Kohls, 1938
13) *Meringis disparilis* Eads, 1979
14) *Meringis facilis* Eads, 1979
15) *Meringis jamesoni* Hubbard, 1943
16) *Meringis nidi* Williams and Hoff, 1951
17) *Meringis parkeri* Jordan, 1937
18) *Meringis rectus* Morlan, 1953
19) *Orchopeas agilis* Rothschild, 1905
20) *Orchopeas leucopus* Baker, 1904
21) *Orchopeas sexdentatus* Baker, 1904
22) *Peromyscopsylla adelpha* Rothschild, 1915
23) *Peromyscopsylla draco* Hopkins, 1951
24) *Peromyscopsylla hesperomys* Baker, 1904
25) *Pleochaetis exilis* Jordan, 1937
26) *Rhadinopsylla multidenticulatus* Morlan and Prince, 1954
27) *Thrassis aridis* Prince, 1944
28) *Thrassis bacchi consimilis* Stark, 1957
29) *Thrassis campestris* Prince, 1944
30) *Thrassis fotus* Jordan, 1925
31) *Thrassis pansus* Jordan, 1925

Anoplura:
32) *Fahrenholzia pinnata* Kellogg and Ferris, 1915
33) *Hoplopleura hesperomydis* (Osborn, 1891)
34) *Hoplopleura hirsuta* Ferris, 1916
35) *Hoplopleura onychomydis* Cook and Beer, 1959
36) *Polyplax auricularis* Kellogg and Ferris, 1915

NM Counties: Bernalillo (3, 14, 17, 31, 35); Chaves (2, 3, 7, 11, 12, 14, 16, 18, 23, 26, 27, 28, 29, 30); Colfax (6, 8, 25); Dona Ana (2, 10, 11, 13); Eddy (30); Hidalgo (10, 27, 31); Lea (11, 21, 30); Luna (3, 9, 10, 13); Roosevelt (11, 20, 24, 25, 27, 30, 32, 33, 34, 36); San Juan (17, 25); Sandoval (11); Santa Fe (1, 4, 5, 15, 16, 17, 18, 19, 20, 21, 25, 26, 27, 28, 31); Socorro (9); Union (1, 5, 22, 23, 25); Valencia (14).

Material Deposited: Flea MSB No.: (**5**) 1016; (**10**) 994, 1032; (**12**) 1024; (**20**) 887; (**25**) 889; (**28**) 881.

Reference: Barnes and others 1977; Eads 1978; Eads and others 1987; Fagerlund and others 2001; Graves and others 1974; Jellison and Senger 1976; Kartman 1960; Kim and others 1986; Morlan 1955; Morlan and Prince 1954; Pfaffenberger and deBruin 1986; Prince 1944; Rail and others 1969; Thomas, 1988; Traub and Hoff 1951; Williams and Hoff 1951.

Genus *Peromyscus*

Host: *Peromyscus boylii* (Baird, 1855) . . . . Brush mouse.
Siphonaptera:
1) *Aetheca wagneri* Baker, 1904
2) *Anomiopsyllus novomexicanensis* Williams and Hoff, 1951
3) *Atyphloceras echis* Jordan and Rothschild, 1915
4) *Atyphloceras multidentatus* C. Fox, 1909
5) *Callistopsyllus terinus* Rothschild, 1905

6) *Catallagia charlottensis* Baker, 1898

7) *Hoplopsyllus anomalus* Baker, 1904

8) *Malaraeus sinomus* Jordan, 1925

9) *Malaraeus telchinum* Rothschild, 1905

10) *Megarthroglossus bisetis* Jordan and Rothschild, 1915

11) *Megarthroglossus divisus* Baker, 1898

12) *Meringis altipecten* Traub and Hoff, 1951

13) *Orchopeas leucopus* Baker, 1904

14) *Peromyscopsylla adelpha* Rothschild, 1915

15) *Plusaetis equatorius asetus* Traub, 1950

16) *Rhadinopsylla sectilis* Jordan and Rothschild, 1923

17) *Stenoponia ponera* Traub and Johnson, 1952

Anoplura:

18) *Hoplopleura hesperomydis* (Osborn, 1891)

NM Counties: Bernalillo (8, 11, 18); Grant (17); Lincoln (14); Los Alamos (14); McKinley (11); Rio Arriba (10, 11, 14); Sandoval (1, 5, 9, 14, 16); Santa Fe (1, 3, 4, 6, 7, 8, 13, 14); Sierra (12); Socorro (14, 15); Valencia (2, 14).

Material Deposited: Flea MSB No.: (**8**) 933; (**14**) 834; (**15**) 831.

Reference: Barnes and others 1977; Eads and others 1987; Fagerlund and others 2001; Haas and others 1973; Holdenried and Morlan 1956; Kim 1965; Mendez 1956; Mendez and Haas 1973; Morlan 1955; Tipton and others 1979; Traub and Hoff 1951; Traub and Johnson 1952.

Host: *Peromyscus eremicus* (Baird, 1858). . . . . Cactus mouse.

Siphonaptera:

1) *Anomiopsyllus hiemalis mexicanus* Holland, 1965

2) *Orchopeas leucopus* Baker, 1904

Anoplura:

3) *Hoplopleura ferrisi* Cook and Beer, 1959

NM Counties: Colfax (1); Grant (3); Socorro (2).

Material Deposited: Flea MSB No.: (**2**) 840.

Reference: Barnes and others 1977; Kim 1965.

Host: *Peromyscus leucopus* (Rafinesque, 1818) . . . . White-footed mouse.

Siphonaptera:

1) *Aetheca wagneri* Baker, 1904

2) *Anomiopsyllus novomexicanensis* Williams and Hoff, 1951

3) *Anomiopsyllus nudata* Baker, 1898

4) *Echidnophaga gallinaceus* Westwood, 1875

5) *Epitedia stanfordi* Traub, 1944

6) *Malaraeus sinomus* Jordan, 1925

7) *Megarthroglossus bisetis* Jordan and Rothschild, 1915

8) *Megarthroglossus divisus* (Baker, 1898)

9) *Meringis bilsingi* Eads and Menzies, 1949

10) *Meringis nidi* Williams and Hoff, 1951

11) *Meringis rectus* Morlan, 1953

12) *Orchopeas agilis* Rothschild, 1905

13) *Orchopeas caedens* Jordan, 1925

14) *Orchopeas leucopus* Baker, 1904

15) *Peromyscopsylla adelpha* Rothschild, 1915

16) *Peromyscopsylla draco* Hopkins, 1951
17) *Peromyscopsylla hesperomys* Baker, 1904
18) *Phalacropsylla hamata* Tipton and Mendez, 1968
19) *Pleochaetis exilis* Jordan, 1937
20) *Rhadinopsylla fraterna* Baker, 1895
21) *Rhadinopsylla multidenticulatus* Morlan and Prince, 1954
22) *Rhadinopsylla sectilis* Jordan and Rothschild, 1923
23) *Thrassis campestris* Prince, 1944
24) *Thrasis fotus* Jordan, 1925
25) *Thrassis pansus* Jordan, 1925

Anoplura:

26) *Hoplopleura hesperomydis* (Osborn, 1891)

NM Counties: Bernalillo (6, 7, 17, 18); Chaves (1, 2, 7, 9, 10, 11, 14, 16, 20, 21, 23, 24); Dona Ana (12); Sandoval (1, 5, 6, 12, 15, 22); Santa Fe (1, 3, 4, 5, 6, 8, 14, 15, 16, 19, 21, 23, 25); Socorro (12).

Material Deposited: Flea MSB No.: (**4**) 765; (**6**) 960; (**12**) 857; (**13**) 785.

Reference: Eads and Campos 1982; Graves and others 1974; Haas and others 1973; Holdenried and Morlan 1955, 1956; Kartman 1960; Kim and others 1986; Morlan 1955; Morlan and Prince 1954; Rail and others 1969; Traub and Hoff 1951.

Host: *Peromyscus maniculatus* (Wagner, 1845). . . . . Deer mouse.

Siphonaptera:

1) *Aetheca wagneri* Baker, 1904
2) *Amardix euphorbae* Rothschild, 1905
3) *Anomiopsyllus hiemalis mexicanus* Holland, 1965
4) *Anomiopsyllus novomexicanensis* Williams and Hoff, 1951
5) *Atyphloceras echis* Jordan and Rothschild, 1915
6) *Callistopsyllus terinus* Rothschild, 1905
7) *Catallagia decipiens* Rothschild, 1915
8) *Epitedia stanfordi* Traub, 1944
9) *Epitedia wnemanni* Rothschild, 1904
10) *Eumolpianus eumolpi* Rothschild, 1905
11) *Foxella ignotus* Baker, 1895
12) *Hystrichopsylla dippiei* Rothschild, 1902
13) *Malaraeus sinomus* Jordan, 1925
14) *Malaraeus telchinum* Rothschild, 1905
15) *Megabothris abantis* Rothschild, 1905
16) *Megarthroglossus bisetis* Jordan and Rothschild, 1915
17) *Megarthroglossus divisus* Baker, 1898
18) *Meringis altipecten* Traub and Hoff, 1951
19) *Meringis arachis* Jordan, 1929
20) *Meringis bilsingi* Eads and Menzies, 1949
21) *Meringis nidi* Williams and Hoff, 1951
22) *Meringis parkeri* Jordan, 1937
23) *Meringis rectus* Morlan, 1953
24) *Orchopeas leucopus* Baker, 1904
25) *Orchopeas sexdentatus* Baker, 1904
26) *Orchopeas sexdentatus neotomae* Auguston, 1943
27) *Peromyscopsylla adelpha* Rothschild, 1915
28) *Peromyscopsylla draco* Hopkins, 1951
29) *Peromyscopsylla hamifer vigens* Jordan, 1937

30) *Peromyscopsylla hesperomys* Baker, 1904

31) *Peromyscopsylla selenis* Rothschild, 1906

32) *Phalacropsylla allos* Wagner, 1936

33) *Rhadinopsylla sectilis* Jordan and Rothschild, 1923

34) *Stenoponia americana* Baker, 1899

35) *Thrassis campestris* Prince, 1944

36) *Thrassis pansus* Jordan, 1925

Anoplura:

37) *Hoplopleura hesperomydis* (Osborn, 1891)

38) *Polyplax auricularis* Kellogg and Ferris, 1915

NM Counties: Bernalillo (1, 4, 7, 13, 16, 17, 33, 37, 38); Dona Ana (20); Hidalgo (4, 5, 18, 19); Otero (21, 24); Rio Arriba (1, 7, 9, 10, 14, 15, 24); San Juan (2); Sandoval (1, 7, 8, 11, 12, 13, 14, 15, 16, 22, 24, 26, 27, 29, 30, 31, 32, 33, 34, 37); Santa Fe (2, 3, 6, 7, 8, 10, 13, 14, 17, 21, 22, 23, 24, 25, 27, 28, 33, 35, 36, 37, 38).

Material Deposited: Flea MSB No.: (**1**) 705; (**2**) 710; (**8**) 725; (**13**) 1001; (**14**) 987; (**15**) 982; (**26**) 852; (**28**) 854.

Reference: Barnes and others 1977; Eads and others 1987; Good 1942; Haas and others 1973; Holdenried and Morlan 1955, 1956; Kim and others 1986; Link 1949; Mendez 1956; Morlan 1955; Traub and Hoff 1951; Williams and Hoff 1951.

Host: *Peromyscus nasutus* (J.A. Allen, 1891) . . . . Northern rock mouse.

Siphonaptera:

1) *Aetheca wagneri* Baker, 1904

2) *Atyphloceras echis* Jordan and Rothschild, 1915

3) *Ceratophyllus vison* Baker, 1904

4) *Epitedia stanfordi* Traub, 1944

5) *Hystrichopsylla dippiei* Rothschild, 1902

6) *Malaraeus sinomus* Jordan, 1925

7) *Megarthroglossus bisetis* Jordan and Rothschild, 1950

8) *Peromyscopsylla adelpha* Rothschild, 1915

9) *Peromyscopsylla hesperomys* Baker, 1904

10) *Rhadinopsylla sectilis* Jordan and Rothschild, 1923

11) *Stenoponia americana* Baker, 1899

Anoplura:

12) *Hoplopleura hesperomydis* (Osborn, 1891)

13) *Polyplax auricularis* Kellogg and Ferris, 1915

NM Counties: Bernalillo (1, 5, 6, 9, 12); Sandoval (11); Santa Fe (1, 2, 3, 4, 6, 7, 8, 10, 12, 13).

Material Deposited: None.

Reference: Holdenried and Morlan 1956; Kim 1965; Kim and others 1986; Morlan 1955; Traub and Hoff 1951; Williams and Hoff 1951.

Host: *Peromyscus* sp.

Siphonaptera:

1) *Aetheca wagneri* Baker, 1904

2) *Anomiopsyllus hiemalis mexicanus* Holland, 1965

3) *Atyphloceras echis* Jordan and Rothschild, 1915

4) *Callistopsyllus terinus* Rothschild, 1905

5) *Epitedia wenmanni* Rothschild, 1904

6) *Malaraeus sinomus* Jordan, 1925

7) *Megarthroglossus bisetis* Jordan and Rothschild, 1915

8) *Megarthroglossus divisus* Baker, 1898

NM Counties: Bernalillo (1, 3, 6, 7, 8); Rio Arriba (2); San Miguel (1, 2, 4); Torrance (5).

Material Deposited: None.

Reference: Barnes and others 1977; Chapin 1919; Jellison and Senger 1976; Mendez 1956; Mendez and Haas 1973; Traub and Hoff 1951.

Host: *Peromyscus truei* (Shufeldt, 1885) . . . . Pinyon mouse.

Siphonaptera:

1) *Aetheca wagneri* Baker, 1904

2) *Amaradix euphorbae* Rothschild, 1905

3) *Anomiopsyllus hiemalis mexicanus* Holland, 1965

4) *Anomiopsyllus novomexicanensis* Williams and Hoff, 1951

5) *Anomiopsyllus nudata* Baker, 1898

6) *Atyphloceras echis* Jordan and Rothschild, 1915

7) *Callistopsyllus terinus* Rothschild, 1905

8) *Catallagia decipiens* Rothschild, 1915

9) *Echidnophaga gallinaceus* Westwood, 1875

10) *Epitedia stanfordi* Traub, 1944

11) *Epitedia wenmanni* Rothschild, 1904

12) *Euhoplopsyllus affinis* Baker, 1904

13) *Hystrichopsylla dippiei* Rothschild, 1902

14) *Malaraeus sinomus* Jordan, 1925

15) *Malaraeus telchinum* Rothschild, 1905

16) *Megabothris abantis* Rothschild, 1905

17) *Megarthroglossus bisetis* Jordan and Rothschild, 1915

18) *Megarthroglossus divisus* Baker, 1898

19) *Meringis nidi* Williams and Hoff, 1951

20) *Meringis rectus* Morlan, 1953

21) *Opisodasys keeni* Baker, 1896

22) *Orchopeas caedens* Jordan, 1925

23) *Orchopeas leucopus* Baker, 1904

24) *Orchopeas sexdentatus* Baker, 1904

25) *Orchopeas sexdentatus neotomae* Auguston, 1943

26) *Oropsylla montanus* Baker, 1895

27) *Peromyscopsylla adelpha* Rothschild, 1915

28) *Peromyscospylla draco* Hopkins, 1951

29) *Peromyscopsylla hesperomys* Baker, 1904

30) *Phalacropsylla allos* Wagner, 1936

31) *Pleochaetis exilis* (Jordan, 1937)

32) *Rhadinopsylla sectilis* Jordan and Rothschild, 1923

33) *Stenistomera alpina* Baker, 1895

34) *Stenistomera macrodactyla* Good, 1942

35) *Thrassis campestris* Prince, 1944

Anoplura:

36) *Hoplopleura hesperomydis* (Osborn, 1891)

37) *Polyplax auricularis* Kellogg and Ferris, 1915

NM Counties: Bernalillo (4, 10, 14, 29, 33); Catron (3); Los Alamos (17); McKinley (31); Rio Arriba (21); Sandoval (1, 6, 7, 8, 10, 13, 14, 15, 17, 18, 23, 25, 27, 28, 29, 32, 33, 34, 35); Santa Fe (1, 5, 6,

7, 9, 10, 12, 14, 17, 18, 19, 20, 23, 24, 26, 27, 28); Socorro (16);
Valencia (4).

Material Deposited: Flea MSB No.: (**1**) 703; (**3**) 707; (**10**) 739; (**11**)
737; (**14**) 932; (**16**) 998; (**18**) 997; (**22**) 827; (**23**) 770; (**31**) 901.

Reference: Barnes and others 1977; Fagerlund and others 2001; Haas
and others 1973; Holdenried and Morlan 1955, 1956; Mendez and
Haas 1973; Morlan 1955; Traub and Hoff 1951.

Genus *Reithrodontomys*

Host: *Reithrodontomys megalotis* (Baird, 1858) . . . . Western harvest mouse.

Siphonaptera:
1) *Aetheca wagneri* Baker, 1904
2) *Echidnophaga gallinaceus* Westwood, 1875
3) *Epitedia stanfordi* Traub, 1944
4) *Malaraeus telchinum* Rothschild, 1905
5) *Megarthroglossus bisetis* Jordan and Rothschild, 1915
6) *Meringis bilsingi* Eads and Menzies, 1949
7) *Meringis nidi* Williams and Hoff, 1951
8) *Meringis rectus* Morlan, 1953
9) *Orchopeas caedens* Jordan, 1925
10) *Orchopeas leucopus* Baker, 1904
11) *Oropsylla montanus* Baker, 1895
12) *Peromyscopsylla adelpha* Rothschild, 1915
13) *Peromyscopsylla draco* Hopkins, 1951
14) *Rhadinopsylla sectilis* Jordan and Rothschild, 1923
15) *Thrassis fotus* Jordan, 1925
16) *Thrassis pansus* Jordan, 1925

Anoplura:
17) *Hoplopleura reithrodontomydis* Ferris, 1951

NM Counties: Chaves (1, 5, 6, 8, 10, 13, 15); McKinley (9); Sandoval
(1, 3, 4, 10, 12, 14, 16); Santa Fe (1, 2, 7, 8, 10, 11, 12, 13); Socorro
(9, 17); Taos (17).

Material Deposited: Flea MSB No.: (**9**) 858; (**12**) 893.

Reference: Graves and others 1974; Haas and others 1973;
Holdenried and Morlan 1955, 1956; Morlan 1955.

Genus *Sigmodon*

Host: *Sigmodon hispidus* Say and Ord, 1825. Hispid cotton rat.

Siphonaptera:
1) *Aetheca wagneri* Baker, 1904
2) *Anomiopsyllus novomexicanensis* Williams and Hoff, 1951
3) *Epitedia wenmanni* Rothschild, 1904
4) *Euhoplopsyllus affinis* Baker, 1904
5) *Euhoplopsyllus glacialis* Taschenber, 1880
6) *Megarthroglossus bisetis* Jordan and Rothschild, 1915
7) *Meringis bilsingi* Eads and Menzies, 1949
8) *Meringis nidi* Williams and Hoff, 1951
9) *Meringis rectus* Morlan, 1953
10) *Orchopeas leucopus* Baker, 1904
11) *Orchopeas sexdentatus* Baker, 1904
12) *Peromyscopsylla draco* Hopkins, 1951
13) *Pleochaetis exilis* Jordan, 1937

14) *Polygenis gwyni* (C. Fox, 1914)

15) *Rhadinopsylla fraterna* Baker, 1895

16) *Rhadinopsylla multidenticulatus* Morlan and Prince, 1954

17) *Thrassis aridis* Prince, 1944

18) *Thrassis campestris* Prince, 1944

19) *Thrassis pansus* Jordan, 1925

Anoplura:

20) *Hoplopleura arizonensis* Stojanovich and Pratt, 1961

21) *Hoplopleura hirsuta* Ferris, 1916

NM Counties: Chaves (1, 2, 3, 4, 6, 7, 8, 9, 10, 11, 12, 14, 15, 16, 18); Roosevelt (5, 10, 13, 17, 21); Socorro (20).

Material Deposited: Flea MSB No.: (**19**) 864.

Reference: Clark and others 1971; Graves and others 1974; Miller and others 1970; Pfaffenberger and deBruin 1988; Rail and others 1969.

Host: *Sigmodon ochrognathus* Bailey, 1902 . . . . Yellow-nosed cotton rat.

Siphonaptera:

Polygenis martinezbaezi Vargas, 1951

NM Counties: Hidalgo.

Material Deposited: None.

Reference: Haas and Wilson 1998.

Family Sciuridae: (Squirrels, Prairie Dogs, and Chipmunks)

Genus *Ammospermophilus*

Host: *Ammospermophilus harrisii* . . . . Harris's antelope squirrel.
(Audubon and Bachman, 1854)

Siphonaptera:

1) *Thrassis pansus* Jordan, 1925

Anoplura:

2) *Enderleinellus suturalis* Osborn, 1891

NM Counties: Bernalillo (2); Santa Fe (2); Socorro (1); Torrance (1).

Material Deposited: Flea MSB No.: (**1**) 813.

Reference: Jellison and Senger 1976; Kim and others 1986; MSB Collection.

Host: *Ammospermophilus leucurus* (Merriam, 1889) . . . . White-tailed antelope squirrel.

Siphonaptera:

Thrassis pansus Jordan, 1925

NM Counties: Socorro.

Material Deposited: Flea MSB No.: 818.

Remarks/Observations: New state host record.

Reference: MSB Collection.

Genus *Cynomys*

Host: *Cynomys gunnisoni* (Baird, 1855) . . . . Gunnison's prairie dog.

Siphonaptera:

1) *Echidnophaga gallinaceus* Westwood, 1875

2) *Hoplopsyllus anomalus* Baker, 1904

3) *Meringis rectus* Morlan, 1953

4) *Oropsylla hirsutus* Baker, 1895

5) *Oropsylla idahoensis* Baker, 1904

6) *Oropsylla labis* Jordan and Rothschild, 1922

7) *Oropsylla montanus* Baker, 1895

8) *Oropsylla tuberculatus cynomuris* Jellison, 1939

9) *Thrassi pansus* Jordan, 1925

10) *Thrassis stanfordi* Wagner, 1936

Anoplura:

11) *Enderleinellus suturalis* Osborn, 1981

12) *Linognathoides citellinus* Ferris, 1942

13) *Neohaematopinus citellinus* Ferris, 1942

NM Counties: Bernalillo (4, 10); Colfax (5, 6, 8); Rio Arriba (4, 10); Sandoval (4, 5, 7, 8); Santa Fe (1, 2, 4, 8, 9, 11, 12, 13); Taos (4); Torrance (4).

Material Deposited: None.

Reference: Fagerlund and others 2001; Haas and others 1973; Holdenried and Morlan 1956; Hopkins and Rothschild 1953; Jellison and Senger 1976; Kim and others 1986; Link 1949; Morlan 1955; Morlan and Hoff 1957; O'Connor and Pfaffenberger 1987.

Host: *Cynomys ludovicianus* (Ord, 1815) . . . . Black-tailed prairie dog.

Siphonaptera:

1) *Oropsylla hirsutus* Baker, 1895

2) *Pulex simulans* Baker, 1895

NM Counties: Chaves (1); Roosevelt (1, 2).

Material Deposited: None.

Reference: Clark and others 1971; Pfaffenberger and others 1984.

Host: *Cynomys* sp.

Siphonaptera:

1) *Meringis parkeri* Jordan, 1937

2) *Oropsylla hirsutus* Baker, 1895

NM Counties: Catron (1, 2).

Material Deposited: None.

Reference: Jellison and Senger 1976.

Genus *Marmota*

Host: *Marmota flaviventris* (Audubon and Bachman, 1841) . . . . . Yellow-bellied marmot.

Siphonaptera:

1) *Thrassis stanfordi* Wagner, 1936

Anoplura:

2) *Linognathoides marmotae* (Ferris, 1923)

NM Counties: Rio Arriba (1); Santa Fe (1, 2).

Material Deposited: None.

Reference: Holdenried and Morlan 1956; Kim and others 1986; Link 1949; Morlan 1955.

Genus *Sciurus*

Host: *Sciurus aberti* Woodhouse, 1853 . . . . Abert's squirrel.

Siphonaptera:

1) *Anomiopsyllus martini* Holland, 1965

2) *Anomiopsyllus nudata* Baker, 1898

3) *Ceratophyllus vison* Baker, 1904

4) *Eumolpianus eumolpi americanus* Hubbard, 1950

5) *Opisodasys robustus* Jordan, 1925

6) *Orchopeas caedens* Jordan, 1925

7) *Orchopeas sexdentatus neotomae* Auguston, 1943

8) *Tarsopsylla coloradensis* Baker, 1895

NM Counties: Catron (1,3,5,6); Sandoval (2,4,5,7,8); Socorro (5,6,7).

Material Deposited: Flea MSB Nos. respectively: (**4**) 1531; (**5**) 1534; (**7**) 1551.

Reference: Barnes 1982; Barnes and others 1977; Haas and others 1973; Jellison 1939; Jordan 1925; Patrick and Wilson 1995.

Host: *Sciurus arizonensis* Coues, 1867 . . . . .Arizona gray squirrel.

Siphonaptera:

Orchopeas fulleri Traub, 1950

NM Counties: Catron.

Material Deposited: None.

Reference: Haas 1973.

Genus *Spermophilus*

Host: *Spermophilus lateralis* (Say, 1823) . . . . Golden-mantled ground squirrel.

Siphonaptera:

1) *Catallagia decipiens* Rothschild, 1915

2) *Eumolpianus eumolpi* Rothschild, 1905

3) *Eumolpianus eumolpi americanus* (Hubbard, 1950)

4) *Hystrichopsylla dippiei* Rothschild, 1902

5) *Malaraeus telchinum* Rothschild, 1905

6) *Megabothris abantis* Rothschild, 1905

7) *Oropsylla hirsutus* Baker, 1895

8) *Oropsylla idahoensis* Baker, 1904

9) *Oropsylla montanus* Baker, 1895

10) *Oropsylla tuberculatus cynomuris* Jellison, 1939

NM Counties: Rio Arriba (5, 8, 10); Sandoval (1, 3, 4, 6, 7, 8, 9); Santa Fe (2, 8, 9).

Material Deposited: None.

Reference: Haas and others 1973; Holdenried and Morlan 1956; Link 1949; Morlan 1955.

Host: *Spermophilus spilosoma* Bennett, 1833 . . . . Spotted ground squirrel.

Siphonaptera:

1) *Aetheca wagneri* Baker, 1904

2) *Echidnophaga gallinaceus* Westwood, 1875

3) *Euhoplopsyllus affinis* Baker, 1904

4) *Hoplopsyllus anomalus* Baker, 1904

5) *Meringis jamesoni* Hubbard, 1943

6) *Meringis nidi* Williams and Hoff, 1951

7) *Meringis parkeri* Jordan, 1937

8) *Meringis rectus* Morlan, 1953

9) *Orchopeas leucopus* Baker, 1904

10) *Thrassis bacchi consimilis* Stark, 1957

11) *Thrassis campestris* Prince, 1944

12) *Thrassis fotus* Jordan, 1925

13) *Thrassis pansus* Jordan, 1925

Anoplura:

14) *Enderleinellus suturalis* Osborn, 1891

15) *Linognathoides spilosomae* Stojanovich and Pratt, 1961

16) *Neohaematopinus citellinus* Ferris, 1942

17) *Neohaematopinus spilosomae* Stojanovich and Pratt, 1961

NM Counties: Bernalillo (2, 8, 13, 14, 15, 16, 17); Chaves (3, 11, 12); Santa Fe (1, 2, 4, 5, 6, 7, 8, 9, 13, 14, 16).

Material Deposited: Flea MSB No.: (**2**) 1599; (**10**) 868; (**13**) 823.

Reference: Graves and others 1974; Holdenried and Morlan 1956; Jellison and Senger 1976; Kim et al, 1986; Rail and others 1969; Williams and Hoff 1951.

Host: *Spermophilus tridecemlineatus* (Mitchill, 1821) . . .Thirteen-lined ground squirrel.

Siphonaptera:

Catallagia neweyi Holland and Loshbaugh, 1958

NM Counties: Colfax.

Material Deposited: None.

Reference: Fagerlund and others 2001.

Host: *Spermophilus variegatus* (Erxleben, 1777) . . . . Rock squirrel.

Siphonaptera:

1) *Anomiopsyllus hiemalis mexicanus* Holland, 1965

2) *Echidnophaga gallinaceus* Westwood, 1875

3) *Hoplopsyllus anomalus* Baker, 1904

4) *Meringis rectus* Morlan, 1953

5) *Orchopeas caedens* Jordan, 1925

6) *Orchopeas leucopus* Baker, 1904

7) *Oropsylla hirsutus* Baker, 1895

8) *Oropsylla idahoensis* Baker, 1904

9) *Oropsylla montanus* Baker, 1895

10) *Thrassis fotus* Jordan, 1925

Anoplura:

11) *Linognathoides laeviusculus* (Grube, 1851)

12) *Neohaematopinus citellinus* Ferris, 1842

NM Counties: Bernalillo (2, 3, 7, 11); Catron (1); Otero (5, 9); Rio Arriba (7); Sandoval (2, 3, 8); Santa Fe (2, 3, 4, 7, 10, 11, 12).

Material Deposited: Flea MSB No.: (**3**) 733; (**6**) 930.

Reference: Barnes and others 1977; Haas and others 1973; Holdenried and Morlan 1955, 1956; Jellison and Senger 1976; Kim and others 1986; Link 1949; Morlan 1955; Williams and Hoff 1951.

Genus *Tamias*

Host: *Tamias dorsalis* Baird, 1855 . . . . .Cliff chipmunk.

Siphonaptera:

Eumolpianus eumolpi americanus Hubbard, 1950

NM Counties: McKinley.

Material Deposited: Flea MSB No.: 717.

Reference: MSB Collection.

Host: *Tamias minimus* Bachman, 1839 . . . . Least chipmunk.

Siphonaptera:

1) *Aetheca wagneri* Baker, 1904

2) *Anomiopsyllus nudata* Baker, 1898

3) *Ceratophyllus vison* Baker, 1904

4) *Eumolpianus eumolpi* Rothschild, 1905

5) *Eumolpianus eumolpi americanus* (Hubbard, 1950)

6) *Hystrichopsylla dippiei* Rothschild, 1902

7) *Megarthroglossus wilsoni* Mendez and Haas, 1973

8) *Oropsylla idahoensis* Baker, 1905

NM Counties: Colfax (7); Sandoval (1, 2, 3, 5, 6, 8); Santa Fe (4).

Material Deposited: None.

Reference: Fagerlund and others 2001; Haas and others 1973; Holdenried and Morlan 1956; Morlan 1955; Tipton and others 1979.

Host: *Tamias quadrivittatus* (Say, 1823) . . . . Colorado chipmunk.

Siphonaptera:

1) *Aetheca wagneri* Baker, 1904

2) *Anomiopsyllus nudata* Baker, 1898

3) *Catallagia decipiens* Rothschild, 1915

4) *Epitedia stanfordi* Traub, 1944

5) *Eumolpianus eumolpi* Rothschild, 1905

6) *Eumolpianus eumolpi americanus* (Hubbard, 1950)

7) *Hystrichopsylla dippiei* Rothschild, 1902

8) *Orchopeas leucopus* Baker, 1904

9) *Oropsylla idahoensis* Baker, 1904

10) *Peromyscopsylla adelpha* Rothschild, 1915

11) *Stenistomera alpina* Baker, 1895

Anoplura:

12) *Hoplopleura arboricola* Kellog and Ferris, 1915

13) *Neohaemotopinus pacificus* Kellogg and Ferris, 1915

NM Counties: Bernalillo (5, 7, 11, 12); Rio Arriba (5, 8); Sandoval (1, 2, 3, 4, 6, 7); Santa Fe (1, 5, 7, 9, 10, 11, 13); Socorro (12).

Material Deposited: None.

Reference: Fagerlund and others 2001; Haas and others 1973; Holdenried and Morlan 1955, 1956; Kim and others 1986; Link 1949; Morlan 1955; Traub and Hoff 1951.

Host: *Tamias* sp.

Siphonaptera:

1) *Eumolpianus eumolpi* Rothschild, 1905

2) *Eumolpi eumolpi americanus* Hubbard, 1950

Anoplura:

3) *Hoplopleura arboricola* Kellogg and Ferris, 1915

4) *Linognathoides pacificus* Kellogg and Ferris, 1915

NM Counties: Bernalillo (3); Otero (1, 2); Santa Fe (4).

Material Deposited: Flea MSB No.: (**1**) 747.

Reference: Jellison and Senger 1976; Kim and others 1986.

Genus *Tamiasciuris*

Host: *Tamiasciurus hudsonicus* (Erxleben, 1777) . . . . Red squirrel.

Siphonaptera:

1) *Aetheca wagneri* Baker, 1904

2) *Amaradix bitterootensis* Dunn, 1923

3) *Catallagia decipiens* Rothschild, 1915

4) *Ceratophyllus vison* Baker, 1904

5) *Eumolpianus eumolpi* Rothschild, 1915

6) *Eumolpianus eumolpi americanus* (Hubbard, 1950)

7) *Hystrichopsylla dippiei* Rothschild, 1902

8) *Malaraeus telchinum* Rothschild, 1905

9) *Megarthroglossus bisetis* Jordan and Rothschild, 1915

10) *Megarthroglossus divisus* Baker, 1898

11) *Opisodasys robustus* Jordan, 1925

12) *Orchopeas caedens* Jordan, 1925

13) *Orchopeas leucopus* Baker, 1904

14) *Orchopeas sexdentatus* Baker, 1904

15) *Orchopeas sexdentatus neotomae* Auguston, 1943

16) *Oropsylla idahoensis* Baker, 1904

17) *Tarsopsylla coloradensis* Baker, 1895

NM Counties: Catron (4, 11, 12, 16); Los Alamos (4); Sandoval (1, 2, 3, 4, 6, 7, 8, 9, 12, 13, 14, 15); Santa Fe (4, 5, 12, 17); Taos (4, 11); Valencia (9).

Material Deposited: Flea MSB No.: (**2**) 1529; (**3**) 1530; (**11**) 1538; (**12**) 1543.

Reference: Haas 1972; Haas and others 1973; Holdenried and Morlan 1956; Mendez and Haas 1973; Morlan 1955; Patrick and Wilson, 1995.

References

Barnes, A. M.; Tipton, V. J.; Wilde, J. A. 1977. The subfamily Anomiopsyllinae (Hystrichopsyllidae: Siphonaptera). I. A revision of the genus *Anomiopsyllus* Baker. Great Basin Naturalist. 37(2): 138-206.

Barnes, A. M. 1982. Surveillance and control of bubonic plague in the United States. Symposia of the Zoological Society of London. 50: 237-270.

Becker, E. R. 1947. Distribution of the tropical rat flea (*Xenopsylla cheopis*) in the interior of the United States. Iowa Academy of Science. 54: 297-299.

Bermudez, F. C.; Stuart, J. N.; Frey, J. K.; Valdez, R. 1995. Distribution and status of the Virginia opossum (*Didelphis virginiana*) in New Mexico. Southwestern Naturalist. 40(3): 336-340.

Brooks, D. R. 1993. Critical Comment: Extending the symbiotype concept to host voucher specimens. Journal of Parasitology. 79: 631-633.

Brown, T. Undated. A guide to the names of animals known to be infected in New Mexico. Unpublished list. New Mexico Environmental Division, Vector Control. 1 p.

Busvine, J. R. 1978. Evidence from double infestations for the specific status of human head lice and body lice (Anoplura). Systematic Entomology. 3: 1-8.

Centers for Disease Control and Prevention. 2003. Imported plague—New York City, 2002. Morbidity and Mortality Weekly Report. 52: 725-728.

Chapin, E. A. 1919. New species of North American Siphonaptera. Bulletin of the Brooklyn Entomological Society. 14(2): 49-62.

Clark, P. H.; Cole, M. M.; Forcum, D. L.; Wheeler, J. R.; Wheeler, K.; Miller, B. E. 1971. Preliminary evaluation of three systemic insecticides in baits for control of fleas of wild rats and rabbits. Journal of Economic Entomology. 64: 1190-1193.

Dryden, M. W.; Broce, A. B. 1993. Development of a trap for collecting newly emerged *Ctenocephalides felis* (Siphonaptera: Pulicidae) in homes. Journal of Medical Entomology. 30: 901-906.

Eads, R. E. 1978. Two new species of fleas of the genus *Meringis* (Siphonaptera: Hystrichopsyllidae). Great Basin Naturalist. 38(4): 447-455.

Eads, R. E.; Campos, E. G. 1982. Description of a new *Phalacropsylla* and notes on *P. allos* (Siphonaptera: Hystrichopsyllidae). Great Basin Naturalist. 42(2): 241-245.

Eads, R. E.; Campos, E. G.; Barnes, A. M. 1979. New records for several flea (Siphonaptera) species in the United States, with observations on species parasitizing carnivores in the Rocky Mountain region. Proceedings of the Entomological Society of Washington. 81(1): 38-42.

Eads, R. E.; Campos, E. G.; Maupin, G. O. 1987. A review of the genus *Meringis* (Siphonaptera: Hystrichopsyllidae). Journal of Medical Entomology. 24(4): 467-476.

Fagerlund, R.; Ford, P. L.; Brown, T.; Polechla, P. J., Jr. 2001. New records for fleas (Siphonaptera) from New Mexico with notes on plague-carrying species. Southwestern Naturalist. 46: 94-95.

Forcum, D. L.; Rael, C. D.; Wheeler, J. R.; Miller, B. E. 1969. Abundance of cottontails and their fleas at Red Bluff Ranch, New Mexico. Journal of Wildlife Management. 33(2): 422-424.

Frey, J. K.; Yates, T. L. 1996. Mammalian diversity in New Mexico. New Mexico Journal of Science. 36: 4-37.

Frey, J. K.; Yates, T. L.; Duszynski, D. W.; Gannon, W. L.; Gardner, S. L. 1992. Designation and curatorial management of type host specimens (symbiotypes) for new parasite species. Journal of Parasitology. 78: 930-932.

Gardner, S. L. 1996. Field parasitology techniques for use with mammals. In: Wilson, D. E., Cole, F. R., Nichols, J. D., Rudran, R., Foster, M. S., eds. Measuring and monitoring biological diversity: standard methods for mammals. Washington, DC: Smithsonian Institution Press. p. 291-298.

Good, N. E. 1942. Key to the males of the genus *Atyphloceras* with a description of the male of *Atyphloceras echis* (Siphonaptera). Pan-Pacific Entomologist. 28(2): 87-90.

Graves, G. N.; Bennett, W. C.; Wheeler, J. R.; Miller, B. E.; Forcum, D. L. 1974. Sylvatic plague studies in southeast New Mexico. Journal of Medical Entomology. 11(4): 488-498.

Haas, G. E. 1972. Partial castration in *Monopsyllus vison* (Baker) (Siphonaptera). Entomological News. 83: 275-278.

Haas, G. E. 1973. Morphological notes on some Siphonaptera (Leptopsyllidae and Ceratophyllidae) of New Mexico. America Midland Naturalist. 90(1): 246-252.

Haas, G.; Wilson, N. 1998. *Polygenis martinezbaezi* (Siphonaptera: Rhopalopsyllidae) reared from a rodent nest found in the Peloncillo Mountains of southwestern New Mexico. Journal of Medical Entomology. 35(4): 431-432.

Haas, G.; Martin, R. P.; Swickard, M.; Miller, B. E. 1973. Siphonaptera-mammal relationships in northcentral New Mexico. Journal of Medical Entomology. 10(3): 281-289.

Harrison, R. L.; Patrick, M. J.; Schmitt, C. G. 2003. Foxes, fleas, and plague in New Mexico. Southwestern Naturalist. In press.

Holdenried, R.; Morlan, H. B. 1955. Plague-infected fleas from northern New Mexico wild rodents. Journal of Infectious Diseases. 96: 133-137.

Holdenried, R.; Morlan, H. B. 1956. A field study of wild mammals and fleas of Santa Fe County, New Mexico. American Midland Naturalist. 55(2): 369-381.

Hopkins, G. H. E.; Rothschild, M. 1953. An illustrated catalogue of the Rothschild collection of fleas (Siphonaptera) in the British Museum (Natural History), Vol. 1 Tungidae and Pulicidae. British Museum of Natural History. 361 p.

Hubbard, J. P.; Schmitt, C. G 1984. The black-footed ferret in New Mexico. Final report to the Bureau of Land Management, Santa Fe, NM. 118 p.

Jellison, W. J. 1939. *Opisodasys* Jordan 1933, a genus of Siphonaptera. Journal of Parasitology. 25: 413-420.

Jellison, W. J.; Senger, S. M. 1976. Fleas of western North America except Montana in the Rocky Mountain laboratory collection. Western Washington State College, Bellingham, WA. p. 55-136.

Johnson, P. T.; Traub, R. 1954. Revision of the flea genus *Peromyscopsylla*. Smithsonian Miscellaneous Collections. 123(4): 1-68.

Jordan, K. 1925. New Siphonaptera. Novitates Zoologicae. 32: 96-112.

Jordan, K.; Rothschild, N. C. 1915. Contribution to our knowledge of American Siphonaptera. Ectoparasites. 1: 45-60.

Kartman, L. 1960. The role of rabbits in sylvatic plague epidemiology, with special attention to human cases in New Mexico and use of the fluorescent antibody technique for detection of Pasteurella pestis in field specimens. Zoonoses Research. 1: 1-27.

Kim, K. C. 1965. A review of the Hoplopleura hesperomydis complex (Anoplura: Hoplopleuridae). Journal of Parasitology. 51(5): 871-887.

Kim, K. C. 1985. Coevolution of parasitic arthropods and mammals. John Wiley and Sons, New York, NY. 800 p.

Kim, K. C.; Pratt, H. D.; Stojanovich, C. J. 1986. The sucking lice of North America, an illustrated manual for identification. Pennsylvania State University Press. 241 p.

Kohls, G. M. 1940. Siphonaptera, a study of the species infesting wild hares and rabbits of North America north of Mexico. United States Public Health Service, National Institutes of Health Bulletin. 175: 1-34.

Laney, L. H. 1950. Annual report, rodent control, New Mexico District. U.S. District. U.S. Fish and Wildlife Service, and New Mexico College of Agriculture and Mechanical Arts, Extension Service. 10 p.

Lechleitner, R. R.; Tileson, J. V.; Kartman, L. 1962. Die-off of a Gunnison's prairie dog colony in central Colorado. 1. Ecological observations and description of the epizootic. Zoonoses Research. 1: 185-199.

Link, V. B. 1949. Plague among wild rodents in Rio Arriba County, New Mexico. American Journal of Tropical Medicine. 29: 493-500.

Marquardt, W. C.; Demaree, R. S.; Grieve, R. B. 2000. Parasitology and vector biology. San Diego, CA: Harcourt Academic Press. 697 p.

Mendez, E. 1956. A revision of the genus Megarthroglossus Jordan and Rothschild 1915 (Siphonaptera: Hystrichopsyllidae). University of California Publications in Entomology. 11: 159-192.

Mendez, E.; Haas, G. E. 1973. A new flea of the genus Megarthroglossus Jordan and Rothschild from New Mexico (Siphonaptera: Hystrichopsyllidae: Anomiopsyllinae). Journal of Medical Entomology. 9(4): 285-288.

Miller, B. E.; Forcum, D. L.; Weeks, K. W.; Wheeler, J. R.; Rail, C. D. 1970. An evaluation of insecticides for flea control on wild mammals. Journal of Medical Entomology. 7: 697-702.

Morlan, H. B. 1955. Mammal fleas of Santa Fe County, New Mexico. Texas Reports on Biology and Medicine. 13(1): 93-125.

Morlan, H. B.; Hoff, C. C. 1957. Notes on some Anoplura from New Mexico and Mexico. Journal of Parasitology. 43(3): 347-351.

Morlan, H. B.; Prince, F. M. 1954. Notes of the subfamily Rhadinopsyllinae Wagner 1930 (Siphonaptera: Hystrichopsyllidae) and description of a new species, Rhadinopsylla multidenticulatus. Texas Reports on Biology and Medicine. 12: 1037-1046.

OConnor, B.; Pfaffenberger, G. S. 1987. Systematics and evolution of the genus Paraceroglyphus and related taxa (Acari: Acaridae) associated with fleas (Insecta: Siphonaptera). Journal of Parasitology. 73(6): 1189-1197.

Patrick, M. J.; Harrison, R. L. 1995. Fleas on gray foxes in New Mexico. Journal of Medical Entomology. 32: 201-204.

Patrick, M. J.; Wilson, W. D. 1995. Parasites of Aberts squirrel (Sciurus aberti) and red squirrel (Tamiasciurus hudsonicus) of New Mexico. Journal of Parasitology. 81(2): 321-324.

Pfaffenberger, G. S.; deBruin, D. 1986. Ectoparasitic overlap between sympatric Dipodomys ordii and Onychomys leucogaster (Rodentia) in eastern New Mexico, USA. Journal of Medical Entomology. 23(2): 201-207.

Pfaffenberger, G. S.; deBruin, D. 1988. Parasites of the hispid cotton rat, Sigmodon hispidus (Cricetinae), and population biology of the cotton rat louse, Hoplopleura hirsuta (Hoplopleuridae: Anoplura), in eastern New Mexico, including an annotated host-parasite bibliography. Texas Journal of Science. 40(4): 369-399.

Pfaffenberger, G. S.; Valencia V. B. 1988. Ectoparasites of sympatric cottontails (Sylvilagus audubonii Nelson) and jack rabbits (Lepus californicus Mearns) from the high plains of eastern New Mexico. Journal of Parasitology. 74(5): 842-846.

Pfaffenberger, G. S.; Wilson, C. 1985. Ectoparasites of vertebrates cohabiting black-tailed prairie dog towns in eastern New Mexico. Journal of Wildlife Diseases. 21: 69-72.

Pfaffenberger, G. S.; Nygren, B.; deBruin, D.; Wilson, C. 1984. Parasites of the black-tailed prairie dog (Cynomys ludovicianus) from eastern New Mexico. Proceedings of the Helminthological Society of Washington. 51(2): 241-244.

Prince, F. M. 1943. Species of fleas on rats collected in states west of the 102nd meridian and their relation to the dissemination of plague. Public Health Reports. 58: 700-708.

Prince, F. M. 1944. Descriptions of three new species of Thrassis Jordan and the females of T. bacchi Rothschild and T. pansus Jordan. Pan-Pacific Entomologist. 20(1): 13-19.

Prince, F. M. 1945. Descriptions of three new species of Dactyopsylla Jordan and one new subspecies of Foxella Wagner, with records of other species in the genera (Siphonaptera). Canadian Entomologist. 77: 15-20.

Rail, C. D.; Forcum, D. L.; Wheeler, J. R.; Miller, B. E. 1969. Wild mammals and fleas of Red Bluff Ranch, New Mexico. Journal of Medical Entomology. 6(1): 92-94.

Roberts, L. S.; Janovy, J., Jr. 2000. Foundations of parasitology (6th ed.). Boston, MA: McGraw-Hill, p. 539-549, 559-569.

Rodriguez, P. H. 1977. A survey of ectoparasites of hares and rabbits in Grant County, New Mexico. Texas Journal of Science. 28: 358.

Rollag, O. J.; Skeels, M. R.; Nims, L. J.; Thilsted, J. P.; Mann, J. M. 1981. Feline plague in New Mexico: report of five cases. AmericanVeterinary Medical Association. 179: 1381-1383.

Service, M. W. 2000. Medical entomology for students (2nd ed.). Cambridge, UK: Cambridge University Press. p. 167-192.

Thomas, R. E. 1988. A review of flea collection records from Onychomys leucogaster with observations on the role of grasshopper mice in the epizoology of wild rodent plague. Great Basin Naturalist. 48: 83-95.

Thomas, R. E. 1996. Fleas and the agents they transmit. In: Beaty, B. J., Marquardt, W. C., eds. The biology of disease vectors. Niwot, CO: University Press of Colorado. p. 146-159.

Tipton, V. J.; Stark, H. E.; Wildie, J. A. 1979. Anomiopsyllinae (Siphonaptera: Hystrichopsyllinae), II. The genera *Callistopsyllus, Conorhinopsylla, Megarthroglossus,* and *Stenistomera*. Great Basin Naturalist. 39(4): 351-418.

Traub, R.; Hoff, C. C. 1951. Records and descriptions of fleas from New Mexico (Siphonaptera). American Museum Novitates. 1530: 1-23.

Traub, R.; Johnson, P. T. 1952. *Kohlsia whartoni* and *Stenoponia ponera*, new species of fleas from North America. Journal of Parasitology. 38: 6-18.

Whitaker, J. O. 1982. Ectoparasites of mammals of Indiana. Indianapolis, IN: Indiana Academy of Sciences. 240 p.

Williams, L. A.; Hoff, C. C. 1951. Fleas from the upper sonoran zone near Albuquerque, New Mexico. Proceedings of the United States National Museum. 101(3278): 305-313.

Zinsser, H. 1934. Rats, lice and history. Boston, MA: Little, Brown and Co. 301 p.

Appendix A. New Mexico Ectoparasites and Their Mammal Hosts

Order Siphonaptera (Fleas)

Family Ceratophyllidae

Aetheca wagneri Baker, 1904
  Bassariscus astutus
  Clethrionomys gapperi
  Dipodomys merriami
  D. ordii
  Microtus longicaudus
  M. montanus
  Mus musculus
  Neotoma albigula
  N. cinerea
  N. mexicana
  N. micropus
  Onychomys leucogaster
  Peromyscus boylii
  P. leucopus
  P. maniculatus
  P. nasutus
  P. truei
  Peromyscus sp.
  Reithrodontomys megalotis
  Sigmodon hispidus
  Spermophilus spilosoma
  Sylvilagus audubonii
  Tamias minimus
  T. quadrivitattus
  Tamiasciurus hudsonicus
Amaradix bitterootensis Dunn, 1923
  Tamiasciurus hudsonicus
Amaradix euphorbae Rothschild, 1905
  Clethrionomys gapperi
  Peromyscus maniculatus
  P. truei
Amphalius necopinus Jordan, 1925
  Ochotona princeps
Ceratophyllus vison Baker, 1904
  Peromyscus nasutus
  Sciurus aberti
  Tamias minimus
  Tamiasciurus hudsonicus

Eumolpianus eumolpi Rothschild, 1905
  Dipodomys merriami
  Microtus sp.
  Neotoma mexicana
  Peromyscus maniculatus
  Spermophilus lateralis
  Sylvilagus sp.
  Tamias minimus
  T. quadrivittatus
  Tamiasciurus hudsonicus
  Thomomys talpoides
Eumolpianus eumolpi americanus Hubbard, 1950
  Microtus longicaudus
  Sciurus aberti
  Spermophilus lateralis
  Tamias dorsalis
  T. minimus
  T. quadrivitattus
  Tamiasciurus hudsonicus
Dactylopsylla bluei Fox, 1909
  Microtus montanus
Dactylopsylla neomexicana Prince, 1945
  Thomomys talpoides
Foxella apachinus C. Fox, 1914
  Vulpes macrotis macrotis
Foxella ignotus Baker, 1895
  Lynx rufus
  Microtus montanus
  Mustela frenata
  Peromyscus maniculatus
  Thomomys bottae
  T. talpoides
  Urocyon cinereoargenteus
  Vulpes macrotis macrotis
Malaraeus sinomus Jordan, 1925
  Bassariscus astutus
  Dipodomys ordii
  Neotoma albigula
  N. mexicana
  Onychomys leucogaster
  Peromyscus boylii
  P. leucopus
  P. maniculatus
  P. nasutus
  Peromyscus sp.
  P. truei

Malaraeus telchinum Rothschild, 1905
  Clethrionomys gaperi
  Microtus longicaudus
  M. montanus
  Neotoma cinerea
  N. mexicana
  Neotoma sp.
  Onychomys leucogaster
  Peromyscus boylii
  P. maniculatus
  P. truei
  Reithrodontomys megalotis
  Spermophilus lateralis
  Tamiasciurus hudsonicus
Megabothris abantis Rothschild, 1905
  Clethrionomys gapperi
  Microtus longicaudus
  M. montanus
  Microtus sp.
  Mustela frenata
  Neotoma mexicana
  Ochotona princeps
  Peromyscys maniculatus
  P. truei
  Spermophilus lateralis
Nosophyllus fasciatus Bosc, 1800
  Rattus norvegicus
Opisodasys keeni Baker, 1896
  Peromyscus truei
Opisodasys robustus Jordan, 1925
  Sciurus aberti
  Tamiasciurus hudsonicus
Orchopeas agilis Rothschild, 1905
  Neotoma albigula
  Onychomys leucogaster
  Peromyscus leucopus
  Sorex preblei
  Vulpes macrotis macrotis
  V. velox velox
Orchopeas caedens Jordan, 1925
  Onychomys arenicola
  Peromyscus leucopus
  P. truei
  Reithrodontomys megalotis
  Sciurus aberti
  Spermophilus variegatus
  Tamiasciurus hudsonicus
  Vulpes macrotis
  V. velox velox
Orchopeas fulleri Traub, 1950
  Sciurus arizonensis

Orchopeas leucopus Baker, 1904
  Dipodomys merriami
  D. ordii
  Neotoma albigula
  N. micropus
  Neotoma sp.
  Onychomys lecuogaster
  Perognathus flavus
  Peromyscus boylii
  P. eremicus
  P. leucopus
  P. maniculatus
  P. truei
  Reithrodontomys megalotis
  Sigmodon hispidus
  Spermphilus spilosoma
  S. variegatus
  Tamias quadrivittatus
  Tamiasciurus hudsonicus
Orchopeas sexdentatus Baker, 1904
  Dipodomys spectabilis
  Neotoma albigula
  N. cinerea
  N. mexicana
  N. micropus
  Neotoma sp.
  Onychomys leucogaster
  Peromyscus maniculatus
  P. truei
  Sigmodon hispidus
  Sylvilagus audubonii
  Tamiasciurus hudsonicus
Orchopeas sexdentatus neotomae Augustson, 1943
  Bassariscus astutus
  Neotoma albigula
  N. cinerea
  N. mexicana
  N. micropus
  Peromyscus maniculatus
  P. truei
  Sciurus aberti
  Tamiasciurus hudsonicus
Oropsylla hirsutus Baker, 1895
  Cynomys gunnisoni
  C. ludovicianus
  Cynomys sp.
  Spermophilus lateralis
  S. variegatus
  Sylvilagus audubonii
Oropsylla idahoensis Baker, 1904
  Cynomys gunnisoni
  Microtus longicaudus

Perognathus flavus
Spermophilus lateralis
S. variegatus
Tamias minimus
T. quadrivattus
Tamiasciurus hudsonicus

Oropsylla labis Jordan and Rothschild, 1922
Cynomys gunnisoni

Oropsylla montanus Baker, 1895
Bassariscus astutus
Cynomys gunnisoni
Dipodomys merriami
Neotoma albigula
Peromyscus truei
Reithrodontomys megalotis
Spermophilus lateralis
S. variegatus
Spilogale gracilis
Sylvilagus sp.
Vulpes macrotis macrotis

Pleochaetis exilis Jordan, 1937
Dipodomys ordii
D. spectabilis
Lepus californicus
Neotoma albigula
N. mexicana
N. micropus
Onychomys leucogaster
Peromyscus leucopus
P. truei
Sigmodon hispidus
Vulpes macrotis macrotis

Spicata bottaceps Hubbard, 1943
Thomomys bottae

Tarsopsyllus coloradensis Baker, 1904
Sciurus aberti
Tamiasciurus hudsonicus

Thrassis aridis Prince, 1944
Bassariscus astutus
Dipodomys ordii
Onychomys leucogaster
Sigmodon hispidus

Thrassis bacchi consimilis Stark, 1957
D. ordii
Neotoma albigula
Onychomys leucogaster
Spermophilus spilosoma

Thrassis campestris Prince, 1944
Dipodomys merriami
D. ordii
D. spectabilis
Neotoma albigula

N. micropus
Neotoma sp.
Onychomys leucogaster
Peromyscus leucopus
P. maniculatus
P. truei
Sigmodon hispidus
Spermophilus spilosoma
Sylvilagus audubonii

Thrassis fotus Jordan, 1925
Dipodomys merriami
D. ordii
D. spectabilis
Neotoma albigula
N. micropus
Neotoma sp.
Onychomys leucogaster
Reithrodontomys megalotis
Spermophilus spilosoma
S. variegatus
Sylvilagus audubonii

Thrassis pansus Jordan, 1925
Ammospermophilus harrisii
A. leucurus
Dipodomys ordii
D. spectabilis
Mustela frenata
Neotoma albigula
N. micropus
Onychomys leucopus
Perognathus flavescens
Peromyscus leucopus
P. maniculatus
Reithrodontomys megalotis
Sigmodon hispidus
Spermophilus spilosoma

Thrassis stanfordi Wagner, 1936
Cynomys gunisoni
Marmota flaviventris
Mustela frenata

Family Ctenophthalmidae

Anomiopsyllus hiemalis Eads and Menzies, 1948
Neotoma albigula

Anomiopsyllus martini Holland, 1965
Sciurus aberti

Anomiopsyllus hiemalis mexicanus Holland, 1965
Dipodomys merriami
Neotoma albigula
N. mexicana
Neotoma sp.

Peromyscus eremicus
  P. maniculatus
  P. truei
  Spermophilus variegatus
***Anomiopsyllus novomexicanus* Williams and Hoff, 1951**
  Dipodomys merriami
  D. ordii
  D. spectabilis
  Neotoma albigula
  N. mexicana
  N. micropus
  Neotoma sp.
  Onychomys leucogaster
  Peromyscus boylii
  P. leucopus
  P. maniculatus
  P. truei
  Sigmodon hispidus
  Sylvilagus audubonii
  Sylvilagus sp.
***Anomiopsyllus nudata* Baker, 1898**
  Neotoma albigula
  N. mexicana
  N. micropus
  Perognathus flavus
  Peromyscus leucopus
  P. truei
  Sciurus aberti
  Spilogale gracilis
  Tamias minimus
  T. quadrivittatus
  Thomomys talpoides
***Callistopsyllus terinus* Rothschild, 1905**
  Peromyscus boylii
  P. maniculatus
  Peromyscus sp.
  P. truei
***Catallagia charlottensis* Baker, 1898**
  Peromyscus boylii
***Catallagia decipiens* Rothschild, 1915**
  Clethrionomys gapperi
  Microtus lonigcaudus
  M. montanus
  Microtus sp.
  Neotoma cinerea
  N. mexicana
  Peromyscus maniculatus
  P. truei
  Spermophilus lateralis
  Tamias quadrivitattus
  Tamiasciurus hudsonicus

***Catallagia neweyi* Holland and Loshbaugh, 1958**
  Spermophilus tridecemlineatus
***Corrodopsylla curvata* Rothschild, 1915**
  Microtus montanus
  Sorex cinereus
***Delotelis telegoni* Jordan, 1937**
  Microtus longicaudus
***Epitedia stanfordi* Traub, 1944**
  Bassariscus astutus
  Neotoma albigula
  N. micropus
  Onychomys leucogaster
  Perognathus flavus
  Peromyscus leucopus
  P. maniculatus
  P. nasutus
  P. truei
  Reithrodontomys megalotis
  Tamias quadrivittatus
***Epitedia wenmanni* Rothschild, 1904**
  Peromyscus sp.
  P. truei
  Sigmodon hispidus
***Megarthroglossus bisetis* Jordan and Rothschild, 1915**
  Bassariscus astutus
  Dipodomys spectabilis
  Microtus longicaudus
  Neotoma albigula
  N. cinerea
  N. mexicana
  N. micropus
  Neotoma sp.
  Ochotona princeps
  Onychomys leucogaster
  Peromyscus boylii
  P. leucopus
  P. maniculatus
  P. nasutus
  Peromyscus sp.
  P. truei
  Reithrodontomys egalotis
  Sigmodon hispidus
  Sylvilagus audubonii
  S. nuttalli
  Sylvilagus sp.
  Tamiasciurus hudsonicus
***Megarthroglossus cavernicolus* Mendez and Haas, 1972**
  Neotoma cinerea
***Megarthroglossus divisus* Baker, 1898**
  Neotoma albigula
  N. cinerea
  N. micropus

Ochotona princeps
Onychomys leucogaster
Peromyscus boylii
P. leucopus
P. maniculatus
Peromyscus sp.
P. truei
Tamiasciurus hudsonicus

Megarthroglossu procus Jordan and Rothschild, 1915
Neotoma albigula

Megarthroglossus wilsoni Mendez and Haas, 1973
Tamias minimus

Meringis altipecten Traub and Hoff, 1951
Dipodomys merriami
D. ordii
D. spectabilis
Neotoma albigula
Onychomys arenicola
O. leucogaster
Peromyscus boylii
P. maniculatus

Meringis arachis Jordan, 1929
Bassariscus astutus
Dipodomys merriami
D. ordii
D. spectabilis
Neotoma albigula
Onychomys leucogaster
Perognathus flavescens
P. flavus
Peromyscus maniculatus

Meringis bilsingi Eads and Menzies, 1949
Dipodomys merriami
D. ordii
D. spectabilis
Neotoma micropus
Neotoma sp.
Onychomys leucogaster
Peromyscus leucopus
P. maniculatus
Reithrodontomys megalotis
Sigmodon hispidus
Sylvilagus audubonii

Meringis dipodomys Kohls, 1938
Dipodomys merriami
D. ordii
D. spectabilis
Neotoma micropus
Neotoma sp.
Onychomys leucogaster
Perognathus flavus
Sylvilagus audubonii

Sylvilagus sp.

Meringis disparilis Eads, 1979
Dipodomys merriami
D. ordii
Onychomys leucogaster

Meringis facilis Eads, 1979
Neotoma micropus
Onychomys leucogaster
Perognathus flavus

Meringis jamesoni Hubbard, 1943
Dipodomys spectabilis
Neotoma albigula
Onychomys leucogaster
Perognathus flavus
Spermophilus spilosoma

Meringis nidi Williams and Hoff, 1951
Dipodomys merriami
D. ordii
D. spectabilis
Neotoma albigula
N. micropus
Neotoma sp.
Onychomys leucogaster
Perognathus flavus
Peromyscus leucopus
P. maniculatus
P. truei
Reithrodontomys megalotis
Sigmodon hispidus
Spermophilus spilosoma
Sylvilagus audubonii
Sylvilagus sp.

Meringis parkeri Jordan, 1937
Cynomys sp.
Dipodomys merriami
D. ordii
D. spectabilis
Microtus sp.
Neotoma albigula
N. micropus
Onychomys leucogaster
Perognathus flavus
Peromyscus maniculatus
Spermophilus spilosoma

Meringis rectus Morlan, 1953
Cynomys gunnisoni
Dipodomys merriami
D. ordii
D. spectabilis
Neotoma albigula
N. micropus
Neotoma sp.

Onychomys leucogaster
Perognathus flavus
Peromyscus leucopus
P. maniculatus
P. truei
Reithrodontomys megalotis
Sigmodon hispidus
Spermophilus spilosoma
S. variegatus
Sylvilagus audubonii
Sylvilagus sp.

Phalacropsylla allos Wagner, 1936
Neotoma cinerea
N. mexicana
Peromyscus maniculatus
P. truei

Phalacropsylla hamata Tipton and Mendez, 1968
Neotoma albigula
Peromyscus leucopus

Phalacropsylla morlani Eads and Campos, 1982
Ochotona princeps

Rhadinopsylla fraterna Baker, 1895
Clethrionomys gapperi
Dipodomys merriami
D. spectabilis
Neotoma cinerea
Neotoma sp.
Peromyscus leucopus
Sigmodon hispidus
Sylvilagus audubonii
Sylvilagus sp.

Rhadinopsylla goodi Hubbard, 1941
Bassariscus astutus

Rhadinopsylla multidenticulatus Morlan and Prince, 1954
Dipodomys merriami
D. ordii
D. spectabilis
Neotoma albigula
N. micropus
Onychomys leucogaster
Peromyscus leucopus
Sigmodon hispidus
Sylvilagus audubonii

Rhadinopsylla sectilis Jordan and Rothschild, 1923
Neotoma albigula
N. cinerea
Peromyscus boylii
P. leucopus
P. maniculatus
P. nasutus
P. truei

Reithrodontomys megalotis

Stenistomera alpina Baker, 1895
Bassariscus astutus
Lynx rufus
Mustela frenata
Neotoma albigula
N. cinerea
N. mexicana
Ochotona princeps
Peromyscus truei
Sylvilagus nuttallii
Tamias quadrivittatus
Vulpes macrotis macrotis

Stenistomera macrodactyla Good, 1942
Neotoma albigula
Peromyscus truei

Stenoponia americana Baker, 1899
Peromyscus maniculatus
P. nasutus

Stenoponia ponera Traub and Johnson, 1952
Peromyscus boylii

Family Hystrichopsyllidae

Atyphloceras echis Jordan and Rothschild, 1915
Bassariscus astutus
Neotoma albigula
N. micropus
Neotoma sp.
Peromyscus boylii
P. maniculatus
P. nasutus
Peromyscus sp.
P. truei

Atyphloceras multidentatus C. Fox, 1909
Peromyscus boylii

Hystrichopsylla dippiei Rothschild, 1902
Microtus longicaudus
M. montanus
Neotoma cinerea
N. mexicana
Peromyscus maniculatus
P. nasutus
P. truei
Spermophilus lateralis
Tamias minimus
T. quadrivittatus
Tamiasciurus hudsonicus

Family Ischnopsyllidae

Myodopsylla gentilis Jordan and Rothschild, 1921
Myotis yumanensis

Myodopsylla nordina **Traub and Hoff, 1951**
   Myotis thysanodes
Sternopsylla texanus **Fox, 1914**
Tadarida brasiliensis

Family Leptopsyllidae

Ctenophyllus armatus **Wagner, 1901**
   Ochotona princeps
   Thomomys talpoides
Odontopsyllus dentatus **Baker, 1904**
   Sylvilagus audubonii
   S. nuttalli
Peromyscopsylla adelpha **Rothschild, 1915**
   Dipodomys ordii
   Microtus longicaudus
   Onychomys leucogaster
   Peromyscus boylii
   P. leucopus
   P. maniculatus
   P. nasutus
   P. truei
   Reithrodontomys megalotis
   Tamias quadrivittatus
Peromyscopsylla draco **Hopkins, 1951**
   Neotoma micropus
   Onychomys leucogaster
   Peromyscus leucopus
   P. maniculatus
   Reithrodontomys megalotis
   Sigmodon hispidus
Peromyscopsylla hamifer vigens **Jordan, 1937**
   Microtus longicaudus
   M. montanus
   M. pennsylvanicus
   Peromyscus maniculatus
Peromyscopsylla hesperomys **Baker, 1904**
   Neotoma albuigula
   Onychomys leucogaster
   Peromyscus leucopus
   P. maniculatus
   P. nasutus
   P. truei
Peromyscopsylla selenis **Rothschild, 1906**
   Microtus longicaudus
   M. montanus
   M. pennsylvanicus
   Peromyscus maniculatus

Family Pulicidae

Ctenocephalides felis **Bouche, 1835**
   Canis familiaris

   Odocoileus hemionus
Echidnophaga gallinaceus **Westwood, 1875**
   Bassariscus astutus
   Cynomys gunnisoni
   Dipodomys merriami
   D. ordii
   D. spectabilis
   Felis catus
   Lepus californicus
   Mephitis sp.
   Neotoma albigula
   N. micropus
   Neotoma sp.
   Onychomys leucogaster
   Peromyscus leucopus
   P. truei
   Rattus norvegicus
   Reithrodontomys megalotis
   Spermophilus spilosoma
   S. variegatus
   Sylvilagus audubonii
   Sylvilagus sp.
   Urocyon cinereoargenteus
   Vulpes velox velox
Euhoplopsyllus affinis **Baker, 1904**
   Dipodomys merriami
   D. spectabilis
   Lepus californicus
   Neotoma sp.
   Perognathus flavus
   Peromyscus truei
   Sigmodon hispidus
   Spermophilus spilosoma
   Sylvilagus audubonii
   S. floridanus
   S. nuttalli
   Sylvilagus sp.
   Urocyon cinereoargenteus
   Vulpes macrotis macrotis
   V. velox velox
   V. vulpes
Euhoplopsyllus glacialis **Taschenberg, 1880**
   Canis familiaris
   C. latrans
   Felis catus
   Lepus californicus
   Lynx rufus
   Sigmodon hispidus
   Sylvilagus audubonii
Hoplopsyllus anomalus **Baker, 1904**
   Cynomys gunnisoni
   Lepus californicus

Neotoma albigula
Peromyscus boylii
Spermophilus spilosoma
S. variegatus
Spilogale gracilis
Sylvilagus sp.

Pulex irritans Linnaeus, 1758
Canis familiaris
Dipodomys spectabilis
Felis catus
Homo sapiens
Sylvilagus audubonii
Sylvilagus sp.
Urocyon cinereoargenteus
Vulpes macrotis
V. velox

Pulex simulans Baker, 1895
Bassariscus astutus
Cynomys ludovicianus
Dipodomys spectabilis
Sylvilagus audubonii
Urocyon cinereoargenteus
Vulpes macrotis macrotis
V. velox velox
V. vulpes

Spilopsyllus inaequalis Baker, 1895
Canis familiaris
C. latrans
Felis catus
Lepus californicus
Lynx rufus
Ochotona princeps
Sylvilagus audubonii
S. floridanus
Urocyon cineroaregenteus
Vulpes macrotis macrotis
V. vulpes

Xenopsylla cheopis Rothschild, 1903
Rattus norvegicus
R. rattus

Family Rhopalopsyllidae

Polygenis gwyni C. Fox, 1914
Dipodomys spectabilis
Neotoma micropus
Neotoma sp.
Sigmodon hispidus
Sylvilagus audubonii
Sylvilagus sp.

Polygenis martinezbaezi Vargas, 1951
Sigmodon ochrognathus

Order Anoplura (Sucking Lice)

Enderleinellus suturalis Osborn, 1891
Ammospermophilus harrisii
Cynomys gunnisoni
Spermophilus spilosoma

Fahrenholzia pinnata Kellogg and Ferris, 1915
Chaetodipus intermedius
Dipodomys merriami
D. ordii
D. spectabilis
Onychomys leucogaster
Perognathus flavus

Fahrenholzia zacatecae Ferris, 1922
Chaetodipus hispidus

Haemodipsus setoni Ewing, 1924
Lepus californicus
Sylvilagus audubonii

Haematopinus asini Linnaeus, 1758
Equus asinus
Equus caballus
Dipodomys merriami

Hoplopleura acanthopus Burmeisterm 1839
Dipodomys spectabilis
Microtus longicaudus

Hoplopleura arboricola Kellogg and Ferris, 1915
Dipodomys ordii
D. spectabilis
Tamias quadrivittatus

Hoplopleura arizonensis Stojanovich and Pratt, 1961
Sigmodon hispidus

Hoplopleura ferrisi Cook and Beer, 1959
Dipodomys ordii
Peromyscus eremicus

Hoplopleura hesperomydis Osborn, 1891
Dipodomys ordii
Microtus longicaudus
Onychomys leucogaster
Peromyscus boylii
P. leucopus
P. maniculatus
P. nasutus
P. truei

Hoplopleura hirsuta Ferris, 1916
Dipodomys ordii
Onychomys leucogaster
Sigmodon hispidus
Sylvilagus audubonii

Hoplopleura onychomydis Cook and Beer, 1959
Onychomys leucogaster

Hoplopleura reithrodontomydis Ferris, 1951
Reithrodontomys megalotis

Linognathus africanus **Kellogg and Paine, 1911**
  Capra hircus
  Ovis aries
Linognathus setosus **von Olfers, 1816**
  Canis familiaris
  Canis latrans
Linognathoides citellinus **Ferris, 1942**
  Cynomys gunnisoni
Linognathoides laeviusculus **Grube, 1851**
  Spermophilus variegatus
Linognathoides marmotae **Ferris, 1923**
  Marmota flaviventris
Linognathoides neotomae **Ferris, 1942**
  Neotoma sp.
Linognathoides spilosomae **Stojanovich and Pratt, 1961**
  Spermophilus spilosoma
Neohaematopinus citellinus **Ferris, 1942**
  Cynomys gunnisoni
  Spermophilus spilosoma
  S. variegatus
Neohaematopinus neotomae **Ferris, 1941**
  Dipodomys ordii
  Neotoma albigula
  N. mexicana
  N. micropus

Neohaematopinus pacificus **Kellogg and Ferris, 1915**
  Tamias quadrivittatus
Neohaematopinus spilosomae **Stojanovich and Pratt, 1961**
  Spermophilus spilsoma
Pediculus humanus **Linnaeus, 1758**
  Homo sapiens
Phthirus pubis **Linnaeus, 1758**
  Homo sapiens
Polyplax auricularis **Kellogg and Ferris, 1915**
  Onychomys leucogaster
  Peromyscus maniculatus
  P. nasutus
  P. truei

Order Mallophaga (Chewing Lice)

Goniodes squamatus **Emerson, 1950**
  Dipodomys ordii
Werneckiella (Bovicola) equi **Denny, 1842**
  Equus asinus
  E. caballus

Appendix B.

New Mexico County Records of Fleas (Siphonaptera)

Bernalillo
Aetheca wagneri
Anomiopsyllus novomexicanensis
A. hiemalis mexicanus
Atyphloceras echis
Catallagia decipiens
Ctenocephalides felis
Echidnophaga gallinaceus
Epitedia stanfordi
Euhoplopsyllus affinis
Eumolpianus eumolpi
Hoplopsyllus anomalus
Hystrichopsylla dippiei
Foxella ignotus
Malaraeus sinomus
Megarthroglossis bisetis
M. divisus
M. arachis
M. bilsingi
M. facilis
M. nidi
M. parkeri
M. rectus
Myodopsylla nordina
Nosopsyllus fasciatus
Orchopeas sexdentatus
O. sexdentatus neotomae
Oropsylla hirsutus
O. montanus
Peromyscopsylla hesperomys
Phalacropsylla allos
P. hamata
Pulex irritans
Pulex simulans
Rhadinopsylla goodi
R. sectilis
Spilopsylla inaequalis
Stenistomera alpina
Thrassis aridis
T campestris
T. pansus
Thrassis stanfordi
Xenopsyllus cheopis

Catron
Anomiopsyllus hiemalis mexicanus

A. martini
Ceratophyllus vison
Meringis parkeri
Opisodasys robustus
Orchopeas caedens
O. fulleri
Oropsylla hirsutus
O. idahoensis

Chaves
Aetheca wagneri
Anomiopsyllus hiemalis mexicanus
A. novomexicanensis
Atyphloceras echis
Echidnophaga gallinaceus
Epitedia wenmanni
Euhoplopsyllus affinis
E. glacialis
Malaraeus telchinum
Megarthroglossus bisetis
M. bilsingi
M. dipodomys
M. facilis
M. nidi
M. rectus
Orchopeas agilis
O. caedens
O. leucopus
O. sexdentatus
O. sexdentatus neotomae
Oropsylla hirsutus
Peromyscopsylla draco
Polygenis gwyni
Pulex irritans
P. simulans
Rhadinopsylla fraterna
R. multidenticulatus
Spilopsylla inaequalis
Thrassis aridis
T. bacchi consimilis
T. campestris
T. fotus
T. pansus

Cibola
None recorded.

Colfax
Anomiopsyllus hiemalis mexicanus
Catallagia neweyi
Malaraeus telchinum
Megabothris megacolpus
Megarthroglossus bisetis
M. divisus
M. wilsoni
Oropsylla tuberculatus cynomuris
O. idahoensis
O. labis
Pleochaetis exilis

Curry
Echidnophaga gallinaceus
Euhoplopsyllus affinis
E. glacialis

DeBaca
Pleochaetis exilis
Pulex irritans

Dona Ana
Anomiopsyllus novomexicanensis
Euhoplopsyllus affinis
Meringis altipectin
M. arachis
M. bilsingi
M. disparilis
M. nidi
M. rectus
Orchopeas agilis

Eddy
Anomiopsyllus hiemalis
Echidnophaga gallinaceus
Meringis altipectin
M. disparilis
M. nidi
Orchopeas caedens
Sternopsylla texanus
Thrassis fotus

Grant
Atyphloceras echis
Echidnophaga gallinaceus
Euhoplopsyllus affinis
Meringis arachis
M. dipodomys
Spilopsyllus inaequalis
Stenoponia ponera

Guadalupe
Megarthroglossus bisetis

Harding
None recorded.

Hidalgo
Anomiopsyllus novomexicanensis
Atyphloceras echis
Echidnophaga gallinaceus
Meringis altipectin
M. arachis
M. nidi
Polygenis martinezbaezi
Thrassis aridis
Thrassis pansus
Xenopsylla cheopis

Lea
Anomiopsyllus hiemalis
Echidnophaga gallinaceus
Euhoplopsyllus affinis
E. glacialis
Meringis bilsingi
M. dipodomys
M. nidi
M. parkeri
Orchopeas agilis
O. caedens
O. sexdentatus
Pulex irritans
P. simulans
Thrassis fotus

Lincoln
Anomiopsyllus novomexicanensis
A. hiemalis mexicanus
Megarthroglossus divisus
Meringis rectus
Peromyscopsylla adelpha

Los Alamos
Aetheca wagneri
Catallagia decipiens
Ceratophyllus vison
Malaraeus telchinum
Megarthroglossus bisetis
Peromyscopsylla adelpha
Pulex irritans

Luna
Anomiopsyllus novomexicanensis
Echidnophaga gallinaceus
Meringis altipectin
M. arachis
M. bilsingi
M. disparilis
Pulex irritans

McKinley
Eumolpianus eumolpi americanus
Foxella apachinus
Megarthroglossus bisetis

USDA Forest Service RMRS-GTR-123. 2004

M. divisus
Orchopeas agilis
O. caedens
Oropsylla montanus
Phalacropsylla hamata
Pleochaetis exilis
Pulex irritans
Spilopsyllus inaequalis
Stenistomera alpina

Mora
None recorded.

Otero
Anomiopsyllus novomexicanensis
Eumolpianus eumolpi
E. eumolpi americanus
Euhoplopsyllus affinis
Megarthroglossus divisus
Meringis bilsingi
M. nidi
M. rectus
Orchopeas caedens
O. leucopus
Oropsylla montanus

Quay
None recorded.

Rio Arriba
Aetheca wagneri
Anomiopsyllus heimalis mexicanus
A. novomexicanensis
Callistopsyllus terinus
Catallagia decipiens
Echidnophaga gallinaceus
Epitedia wenmanni
Euhoplopsyllus affinis
Eumolpianus eumolpi
E. eumolpi americanus
Foxella ignotus
Malaraeus telchinum
Megabothris abantis
Megarthroglossus bisetis
M. divisus
Meringis parkeri
Opisodasys keeni
Orchopeas leucopus
O. sexdentatus
O. sexdentatus neotomae
Oropsylla hirsutus
O. idahoensis
O. tuberculatus cynomuris
Peromyscopsulla adelpha
Pulex irritans
Spilopsyllus inaequalis

Thrassis pansus
T. stanfordi

Roosevelt
Euhoplopsyllus affinis
E. glacialis
Meringis bilsingi
Orchopeas leucopus
Oropsylla hirsutus
Peromyscopsylla hesperomys
Pleochaetis exilis
Pulex irritans
P. simulans
Thrassis aridis
T. fotus

San Juan
Amaradix euphorbae
Anomiopsyllus novomexicanensis
Meringis parkeri
M. rectus
Pleochaetis exilis
Pulex simulans
Spilopsylla inaequalis

San Miguel
Aetheca wagneri
Atyphloceras echis
Callistopsyllus teinus
Dactylopsylla bluei
D. neomexicana
Megarthroglossus bisetis
Peromyscopsylla hamifer vigens
P. selenis

Sandoval
Aetheca wagneri
Amaradix bitterootensis
A. vonfintelis
Anomiopsyllus nudata
Atyphloceras echis
Callistopsylla terinus
Catallagia decipiens
Ceratophyllus vison
Corrodopsylla curvata
Echidnophaga gallinaceus
Epitedia stanfordi
Euhoplopsyllus affinis
E. glacialis
Eumolpianus eumolpi americanus
Foxella ignotus
Hoplopsyllus anomalus
Hystrichopsylla dippiei
Malaraeus sinomus
M. telchinum
Megabothris abantis

Megarthroglssus bisetis
M. cavernicolus
M. procus
Meringis bilsingi
M. dipodomys
M. jamesoni
M. parkeri
M. rectus
Odontopsyllus dentatus
Opisodasys robustus
Orchopeas agilis
O. caedens
O. leucopus
O. sexdentatus
O. sexdentatus neotomae
Oropsylla hirsutus
O. idahoensis
O. montanus
O. tuberculatus cynomuris
Peromyscopsylla adelpha
P. draco
P. hamifer vigens
P. hesperomys
P. selenis
Phalacropsylla allos
Pulex irritans
Rhadinopsylla fraterna
R. sectilis
Spicata rara
Spilopsyllus inaequalis
Stenistomera alpina
S. macrodactyla
Stenoponia Americana
Tarsopsylla coloradensis
Thrassis campestris
T. pansus

Santa Fe

Aetheca wagneri
Amaradix euphorbae
Amphalius necopinus
Anomiopsyllus hiemalis mexicanus
A. nudata
Atyphloceras echis
A. multidentatus multidentatus
Callistopsylla terinus
Catallagia decipiens
C. charlottensis
Ceratophyllus vison
Ctenocephalides felis
Ctenophyllus armatus
Delotelis telegoni
Echidnophaga gallinaceus

Epitedia stanfordi
Euhoplopsyllus affinis
Eumolpianus eumolpi americanus
Foxella ignotus
Hoplopsyllus anomalus
Hystrichopsylla dippiei
Malaraeus sinomus
M. telchinum
Megabothris abantis
Megarthroglssus bisetis
M. divisus
Meringis arachis
M. jamesoni
M. nidi
M. parkeri
M. rectus
Myodopsylla gentilis
Odontopsyllus dentatus
Orchopeas agilis
O. caedens
O. leucopus
O. sexdentatus
O. sexdentatus neotomae
Oropsylla hirsutus
O. idahoensis
O. montanus
O. tuberculatus cynomuris
Peromyscopsylla adelpha
P. draco
P. hamifer vigens
P. selenis
Phalacropsylla morlani
Pleochaetis exilis
Pulex irritans
Rhadinopsylla fraterna
R. multidenticulatus
R. sectilis
Spicata bottaceps
Spilopsyllus inaequalis
Stenistomera alpina
S. macrodactyla
Tarsopsylla coloradensis
Thrassis aridis
T. bacchi consimilis
T. campestris
T. fotus
T. pansus
T. stanfordi

Sierra

Anomiopsyllus novomexicanensis
Meringis altipectin
M. arachis

M. bilsingi
M. parkeri

Socorro

Anomiopsyllus hiemalis mexicanus
A. novomexicanensis
Ctenophthalmus pseudagyrtes
Echidnophaga gallinaceus
Euhoplopsyllus affinis
Eumolpianus eumolpi
Foxella ignotus
Hystrichopsylla dippei
Malaraeus sinomus
Megabothris abantis
Meringis altipectin
M. arachis
M. parkeri
Opisodasys robustus
Orchopeas agilis
O. caedens
O. leucopus
O. sexdentatus neotomae
O. montanus
Pleochaetis exilis
Plusaetis equatorius asetus
Pulex irritans
P. simulans
Spilopsyllus inaequalis
Thrassis bacchi consimilis
T. pansus

Taos

Anomiopsylla hiemalis mexicanus
Ceratophyllus vison
Opisodasy robustus
Oropsylla hirsutus

Torrance

Epitedia wenmanni
Euhoplopsyllus affinis
Meringis rectus
Oropsylla hirsutus
Pulex irritans
Thrassi pansus

Union

Aetheca wagneri
Malaraerus sinomus
Peromyscopsylla adelpha
P. draco
Pleochaetis exilis
Pulex irritans

Valencia

Anomiopsyllus hiemalis mexicanus
A. novomexicanensis
Megarthroglossus bisetis

Meringis facilis
M. rectus
Nosopsyllus fasciatus
Peromyscopsylla adelpha

New Mexico County Records of Lice
Order Anoplura and Order Mallophaga (as noted)

Bernalillo
Enderleinellus suturalis
Fahrenholzia pinnata
F. zacatecae
Goniodes squamatus (O. Mallophaga)
Hoplopleura arboricola
H. onychomydis
H. hesperomydis
Linognathus africanus
L. setosus
Linognathoides laeviusculus
L. neotomae
L. spilosomae
Neohaematopinus citellinus
N. neotomae
N. spilosomae
Pediculus humanus
Phthirus pubis
Polyplax auricularis

Catron
Fahrenholzia zacatecae

Chaves
Fahrenholzia zacatecae

Cibola
Fahrenholzia zacatecae

Colfax
Fahrenholzia zacatecae

Curry
Fahrenholzia zacatecae
Haemodipsus setoni

DeBaca
Fahrenholzia zacatecae

Dona Ana
Fahrenholzia zacatecae

Eddy
Fahrenholzia zacatecae

Grant
Fahrenholzia zacatecae
Hoplopleura ferrisi

Guadalupe
Fahrenholzia zacatecae

Harding
Fahrenholzia zacatecae

Hidalgo
Fahrenholzia zacatecae

Lea
Fahrenholzia zacatecae

Lincoln
Fahrenholzia zacatecae

Los Alamos
Fahrenholzia zacatecae

Luna
Fahrenholzia zacatecae

McKinley
Fahrenholzia zacatecae

Mora
Fahrenholzia zacatecae

Otero
Fahrenholzia pinnata
Haematopinus asini
Werneckiella (Bovicola) equi (O. Mallophaga)

Quay
Fahrenholzia zacatecae

Rio Arriba
Fahrenholzia zacatecae

Roosevelt
Fahrenholzia pinnata
Fahrenholzia zacatecae
Hoplopleura hesperomydis
H. hirsuta
Polyplax auricularis

San Juan
Fahrenholzia zacatecae

San Miguel
Fahrenholzia zacatecae

Sandoval
Fahrenholzia zacatecae
Hoplopleura hesperomydis

Santa Fe
Enderleinellus suturalis
Fahrenholzia zacatecae
Hoplopleura acanthopus
H. arboricola
H. hesperomydis
Linognathoides citellinus
L. laeviusculus
L. marmotae
L. neotomae
L. pacificus
Neohaematopinus citellinus
N. neotomae

N. pacificus
Polyplax auricularis

Sierra
Fahrenholzia zacatecae

Socorro
Fahrenholzia zacatecae
Hoplopleura arboricola
H. arizonensis
H. reithrodontomydis

Taos
Fahrenholzia zacatecae
Hoplopleura reithrodontomydis

Torrance
Fahrenholzia zacatecae

Union
Fahrenholzia zacatecae

Valencia
Fahrenholzia zacatecae